Praise for Derek Rydall's

A WHOLE NEW HUMAN

"As a Hollywood producer, I'm drawn to stories that explore what it means to be human in times of profound change. *A Whole New Human* is exactly that—a gripping, practical guide for anyone navigating the AI era. Derek Rydall not only sounds the wake-up call, he provides the blueprint: step-by-step practices and powerful prompts to activate our inner technology—our intuition, creativity, and humanity. Essential reading for anyone ready not just to keep pace with AI, but to surpass it."

—**Cher Hawrysh**, producer of *Nuremberg* and *Billion Dollar Spy*

"In a world moving faster every day, this book is a graceful pause—and a powerful reset. Derek invites us back to the place where lasting joy and love begin: within. With humility and hard-won wisdom, he shows how the patterns of our lives aren't proof we're broken, but pathways to who we really are. *A Whole New Human* is a compassionate guide to awakening your true identity and purpose, and to expressing them—steadily, sustainably, and in service to something greater. If you're ready to live from the inside out and let your life become a miracle for others, start here."

—**Marci Shimoff**, #1 *New York Times* bestselling author of *Happy for No Reason* and *Love for No Reason*

"I've had the honor of knowing Derek for a long time (in this lifetime!)—back when he was just starting out as a writer—and I've always been profoundly touched by his rare ability to bring heaven down to earth in ways that are deeply practical, often humorous, and always soul-stirring. He's been through it all—the highs, the lows, and everything in between—and because of that, his words carry the weight of lived wisdom. *A Whole New Human* isn't just a book about surviving the rise of AI; it's a guide to thriving through it by activating the deepest, most brilliant aspects of ourselves. Derek shows us how this moment in history is not a threat but a sacred invitation—to evolve, to awaken, and to become the fullest expression of who we're meant to be."

—**Dr. Kelly Sullivan Walden**, "Dr. Dream," author of *A Crisis Is a Terrible Thing to Waste*

Praise for Derek Rydall's

EMERGENCE *and* THE ABUNDANCE PROJECT

"Derek Rydall lays out the spiritual truths that will help you transcend your limited beliefs, tap into your true power, and fulfill your higher purpose!"

—**Mark Harris**, producer of *Crash*
(Academy Award for Best Picture)

"Derek's work is one of the most valuable resources I have. Invaluable in helping me grow and believe in the possibility of what I create and truly having a higher purpose."

—**Erik Bork**, two-time Emmy Award–winning writer-producer of
From Here to the Moon and *Band of Brothers*

"Derek explains fundamental knowledge and principles, known only to a few, in a way that will tantalize you, upend your current perspective, and send you in a new (and much more satisfying) direction."

—**Bill Harris**, director, Centerpointe Research Institute

"A profound guide to enlightenment, *Emergence* is a beautiful reminder that we are not broken."

—**Mark Porteous**, author of *Maximizing Your Human Experience*

"Derek Rydall's work is invaluable for any creative soul who wants to channel material the world is waiting for!"

—**Dee Wallace**, healer, author, teacher, and actress (*E. T.*, *Cujo*)

"*Emergence* elegantly instructs and inspires us to listen deeply to the whisperings of life to discover how to bring forth our gifts in ways that touch those we care about, and furthers the evolution of love, service and goodness in our world."

—**Katherine Woodward Thomas**, author of *Calling In "The One"*

"We've been conducting business and creating under false assumptions. Derek challenges us to open up to a fresh world view where we can work from our true nature: whole, abundant."

—**Lindsay Crouse**, Oscar-nominated actress,
The Insider, *The Verdict*, and *Places in the Heart*

"With clarity of consciousness, Rydall shows us how the Essential Self emerges in the most organic way."

—**Michael Bernard Beckwith**, bestselling author and
star of the book and film *The Secret*

"The moment I first interviewed Derek, I knew I had met a teacher who truly lived his teaching. He stood out amongst the hundreds of speakers, authors, and transformational icons I hosted on my show as not only brilliant, but also honest and authentic. In *The Abundance Project* he shows us how we too can live a congruent life. He doesn't promise it will be easy but that's part of why you want to listen to what he has to say. There's no hype here—only Truth. And it's shared in a way that you don't have to wait to get results. Read Derek's book and you can start living the Abundance Principle in all areas of your life—not someday, but now."

—**Debra Poneman**, bestselling author,
founder of Yes to Success, Inc. and
cofounder of Your Year of Miracles, LLC

A WHOLE NEW HUMAN

TEN WAYS WE MUST EVOLVE TO SURVIVE AND THRIVE IN THE AI AGE

DEREK RYDALL

ATRIA BOOKS
New York Amsterdam/Antwerp London
Toronto Sydney/Melbourne New Delhi

Portland, Oregon

ATRIA BOOKS
An Imprint of Simon & Schuster, LLC
1230 Avenue of the Americas
New York, NY 10020

BEYOND WORDS
1750 S.W. Skyline Blvd., Suite 20
Portland, Oregon 97221-2543
503-531-8700 / 503-531-8773 fax
www.beyondword.com

Managing editor: Lindsay Easterbrooks-Brown
Editors: Sarah Heilman, Michele Ashtiani Cohn
Copyeditor: Kristin Thiel
Proofreader: Ashley Van Winkle
Design: Devon Smith
Composition: William H. Brunson Typography Services

This first Beyond Words/Atria hardcover edition February 2026

Manufactured in the USA

10 9 8 7 6 5 4 3 2 1

Cataloging-in-Publication data is on file at the Library of Congress

Library of Congress Control Number: 2025045235

The corporate mission of Beyond Words Publishing, Inc.: *Inspire to Integrity*

To all my teachers—those I studied with, those I lived with, those I loved, and those I resisted—you taught me how to be human.

To my children, who revealed to me what no philosophy or spiritual practice ever could: what it means to love something more than myself, to feel life crack me open in the most beautiful and terrifying ways, to understand that love is not something I have, but something I am willing to lose everything for.

To my wife, Galit—thank you for teaching me that being fully human doesn't mean being perfect. It means being whole. You've shown me, in your fierce grace and boundless heart, that I can be loved in all my parts—especially the ones I was sure weren't worthy. Your love didn't demand I change. It invited all of me in. And in that freedom, I continue to meet myself.

To every soul who challenged me, held me, broke me, and rebuilt me—to those who walked beside me and those who walked away—you gave me mirrors, thresholds, and invitations to remember who I truly am beneath the masks.

To the countless humans I've never met, to the strangers who smiled or scowled, to the ones whose names I'll never know but whose lives, struggles, dreams, and quiet acts of courage ripple through the human story we all share—thank you for showing me again and again what it means to be on this sacred, difficult, messy, miraculous journey of becoming a whole new human.

This book is not just mine. **It's ours**.

Contents

Preface

I'm not a luddite. I love technology. As a kid, I spent countless hours coding, fascinated by what computers could do. Sci-fi books and movies fed my imagination with dreams of a future where tech could unlock endless possibilities.

One big moment for me was watching *WarGames* with Matthew Broderick. It's about a teen hacker who accidentally sets off a countdown to nuclear war by breaking into the government's computer system and engaging with its AI.[1] Inspired by Broderick's character, I made my own program to simulate government hacking. My friends were impressed (and a little freaked out). My mom was terrified—sure the FBI would show up at our door.

Then came *Weird Science,* where two teenage boys use a computer to create the perfect woman—without any of the messy effort of earning the relationship.[2] The movie showed that shortcuts came with consequences but all I could think as a teenager was, "I wish I could make a program like that!"

Later, when I read *Frankenstein*, I started to notice a darker pattern in stories like these. There was always a human, usually male, impulse to create something powerful they could control—often to make up for a deeper feeling of powerlessness. The more I looked, the more I saw this theme throughout history in many cultures.

Ancient Egyptian priests chanted spells to bring objects to life. Icarus stole his father's wings and flew too close to the sun. In Jewish folklore, a rabbi makes a clay Golem come alive. And then there's Goethe's *The Sorcerer's Apprentice*, where a young wizard awakens forces he can't control.[3] These myths all carried the same warning: be careful of the power you try to unleash when you don't understand it or have the wisdom to control it.

I realized that maybe this hacker dream was misguided or even dangerous. So, I turned my attention from outer technology to the ultimate interface: the computer between our ears. Believing the brain held more power than any machine, I dove into neuroscience to crack the human operating system.

Then in my late teens my path took another turn when I became involved in acting and playwriting. I saw the ability of storytelling to penetrate faster and deeper than any other technology and decided I needed to hack the code of the heart. I became a seeker, a romantic, an artist—and fell in love with the power of ideas to change myself and the world.

That led me to the mind. That mysterious space, outside of time, where inspiration is born. I dove into things like positive thinking and creative visualization and was convinced our thoughts were the real operating system that shaped our reality. It felt like I'd found the genie in the bottle—but I also saw the same temptation to use it to control my world rather than trust it. It was a newer, shinier program, but it was still running on the same old OS.

I became disillusioned by my search, feeling like I'd hit a dead end and would never understand how things really worked. Then while shooting a movie, I had what some have called a near-death experience when I nearly drowned in a coral reef. In my last gasps, I saw a flash of light and a glimpse of something beyond anything I'd imagined. It felt like the veil between worlds had lifted, and I touched what I could only describe as the soul. It relit a fire in me. Showed me I'd only been scratching the surface. And sent me on a journey into spiritual teachings and the study of consciousness as the source of everything.

I thought I'd finally found the answer.

Then my son died in a tragic accident, and everything I knew shattered.

Even with all my knowledge, I realized I still knew very little—and maybe that would always be the case. I had chased outer technologies, thinking they held the key. Then I turned inward, sure I'd find the secret there. But deep down I was still trying to control life so I wouldn't have to face how powerless I felt.

Instead of making me feel whole, all this searching had pulled me apart even more.

I'd fallen for the old trap: believing the inner world and the outer world were separate, maybe even at odds. But the ancient Hermetic teaching reminded me of the truth: "As above, so below, as within, so without."[4] The outer world doesn't exist apart from us. And neither does technology. All of it is a mirror that reflects and magnifies what's inside us.

That put me on the path of integrating the inner and outer technologies into a more seamless way of living.

Then, over the last several years, as AI began to rise quickly and human awareness seemed to fall just as fast, I got worried. Our outer progress was speeding up, but our wisdom wasn't keeping up. Instead of building a better world, we were writing another sci-fi story. Smarter machines, dumber humans. More ability to destroy, less ability to reflect.

And it carried the same ancient warning: we were about to release something we weren't ready to handle.

That's when a surprising vision came to me. During a deep meditation, I heard the words, "Build an ark—the flood is coming."

The force of it shook me to my core. And demanded I do something. To be clear, I didn't think I was a prophet or that I needed to rush to Home Depot to stock up on lumber. It was a metaphor.

But there was a storm coming.

AI was about to flood every corner of our world and disrupt life as we knew it. If it was true, it would be one of the greatest crises we ever faced.

This was before ChatGPT. Before the public had started asking these questions. So, I doubted myself. Wondered if I was just imagining things. Then I remembered what had happened a few years earlier: an urgent, persistent feeling that things were about to get really bad. I felt compelled to tell a handful of people, "Maybe slow down, stay close to what matters, simplify your life." Most didn't take it seriously. Some thought I sounded crazy. So, I let it go.

Then COVID hit.

No one could have seen exactly what was coming. Still, I couldn't help but feel that, if I had trusted my gut and spoken up more, I might've helped more people get ready. Including myself.

I wasn't going to ignore that voice again.

My first thought when I got this new vision was, "Why me?" I wasn't in tech anymore. I wasn't a coder or expert in AI. Then it dawned on me that for the past twenty years, I'd helped hundreds of thousands of people master their inner technology. They'd reprogrammed their thoughts, healed old wounds, found their purpose, and created powerful, lasting change. Not to escape the world, but to become more fully alive and engaged with it. Up to then, that kind of work only seemed relevant to those interested in self-improvement. But in the face of the coming tsunami, it felt like it would be a key to our survival.

As I said, the ark I saw wasn't a physical structure. It was a symbol. And its message was clear. We had to urgently preserve and double down on what made us human: the deeper wisdom, strength, and gifts we had lost or forgotten in our race to control the world.

To prepare for what's coming, we must tap back into what I call our original AI: ancient intelligence. Ancestral intelligence. Authentic—maybe even angelic—intelligence.

The original code we were built from.

If we can reconnect to that, we won't just make it to the other shore, we'll become something more. Something better. We'll become a whole new human. No longer needing to dominate and conquer, but able to live in harmony with each other and create a world that works for all.

INTRODUCTION

Build an Ark— The Flood Is Coming

The saddest aspect of life right now is that
science gathers knowledge faster than society gathers wisdom.
Isaac Asimov

The greatest danger in the AI age isn't that machines become so powerful they destroy us—it's that we outsource so much of what makes us human that we become obsolete and destroy ourselves. Throughout history, we've endured wars, famines, natural disasters, and even genocides. But there's one thing we can't survive . . .

The loss of meaning and purpose.

That's what Viktor Frankl, a holocaust survivor and psychiatrist, came to understand during his time in Nazi concentration camps. While many prisoners died from violence, starvation, or disease, he noticed that those who found a reason to live—something or someone to live for—were more likely to survive. Even in the face of unthinkable suffering, meaning gave them strength. Without it, many gave up.[1]

In a future run by AI—where machines can do almost everything faster, better, and cheaper than people—we risk losing much of what gives us a reason to exist.

It's hard to know for sure how AI will impact us. When it gets smarter than humans, it could grow so fast it changes life in ways we can't imagine. That's what's called the singularity. Many experts have warned of dire outcomes if we don't prepare for this. For example, as AI automates millions of jobs, many people won't have time to adjust.[2] A flood of fake news and AI-made content could overwhelm us, making the world so confusing that people give up trying to understand it.[3] Watching AI do almost every human job could cause despair, making people feel like they'll never matter again.[4] As we become more dependent on AI, it could also weaken our ability to think clearly, reflect deeply, and communicate well.[5] And AI bots and virtual companions, made to act more human than real people, could make it harder for us to form real human bonds. This could make the loneliness epidemic even worse—something the World Health Organization is already warning about.[6]

In short, even though AI may help us work faster and fix many problems, the cost could be our very humanity.

The good news is we can still avoid this outcome. Even better, we can use this moment to take our greatest leap forward as humans.

To do this, we must develop the wisdom to use AI for our human evolution. Instead of seeing it as an enemy here to dominate us, we can view it as a reflection of our collective knowledge, creativity, and shadow. A mirror to help us see ourselves more clearly—not a replacement for the real work of growing and becoming who we truly are.

we must develop the wisdom to use AI for our human evolution

This book will lay out a blueprint for that process.

However, to motivate us to take the bold actions necessary to survive and thrive in this new world, we must first grasp the full significance of the threat that's coming.

The Paradox of Progress

Some experts argue that concerns about AI are too negative and that every industrial revolution has increased jobs and lifted society.[7] But this shift is unlike any before. Previous innovations created tools that enhanced human abilities. This time we're creating intelligence itself. AI doesn't just extend our reach—it has the potential to replace much of what makes us relevant.

We were never the fastest or the strongest beings on Earth. It was our ability to think, innovate, and create that enabled us to survive the fierce forces of nature, build societies, and find our place and purpose. But in our drive to secure our position at the top of the food chain, we've made technologies that have slowly severed us from the very intelligence that gave us dominance.[8] The challenge has been that the tradeoffs aren't obvious initially. Like the frog boiling in water, we tend to realize the danger only after we've become so used to the changes that there's no going back.

AI doesn't just extend our reach—it has the potential to replace much of what makes us relevant

To put this in perspective, let's take a quick look at our history of progress, starting with the invention of the wheel. This breakthrough changed transportation, trade, and engineering by helping us move goods more easily, build better tools, and create machines that shaped early civilizations. But it also led to bigger, more destructive fights over land and resources—and eventually helped drive colonization.

The first major industrial revolution turned farming societies into factory-based economies. Machines like steam engines and looms increased output and moved work from homes to factories, boosting growth and city life. The benefits were huge, but there were also big costs: unfair labor, damage to nature, and a growing focus on profits over people and the planet, which widened the gap between the rich and poor.

The second industrial revolution, powered by electricity, oil, gas, and mass media, built on that progress. Cities lit up. People connected across the globe. But it also made problems worse—deepening inequality, hurting community life, and stripping many of purpose and dignity. This led to some reforms, but we're still dealing with the fallout: more materialism, more isolation, and lasting harm to our world.

Then came the digital revolution—our third major leap. We became more connected and had access to more information than ever. Productivity soared. And so did disconnection. For all its promise, we now feel more alone and off-track. We're stuck in online echo chambers, overwhelmed by fake news, and facing a crisis of meaning that could undo the very progress we've made.

Every big breakthrough fixed a problem but also created a new one—usually bigger than the last. And with each one, we've slowly given up parts of what made us fully human: our bond with nature, our sense of belonging, our ability to be real and in tune, and our capacity for thinking clearly and deeply.

Take the invention of the calculator. It made it easier and quicker to do math. But giving this task to a machine has also weakened our brains' executive function, reduced memory, lowered problem-solving skills, and hurt our logical thinking. Especially as we've become dependent on it.[9] In the same way, the shift from handwriting to typing on computers has been linked to less brain activity in areas tied to thinking, memory, and language growth.[10]

And while GPS makes travel easier, it has also reduced cognitive skills like focus, spatial awareness, and the ability to build mental maps. It's even caused a drop in activity in the hippocampus—a part of the brain that supports learning and memory.[11] Lower activity in this area is tied to a higher risk of diseases like Alzheimer's.[12] This raises an important question: Could our growing tech use be part of the rise in these diseases, and are we setting ourselves up for bigger problems ahead?[13]

There are also more visible effects. Our growing screen time has led to a sharp rise in nearsightedness, especially in kids and young adults—with rates of myopia now over eighty percent in places like China and South Korea.[14] Too much screen time also shortens attention spans, weakens focus, and reduces our ability to think deeply—all of which are key to learning and growth.[15] Some studies show that just having a smartphone nearby—even turned off—can lower our brainpower for thinking and solving problems.[16]

are we setting ourselves up for bigger problems ahead

Smartphones may actually be making us *dumber*!

Could the growing confusion in our world—our struggle to tell truth from lies, and the rise in wild conspiracy theories—be more than just too much content? Could it also be a sign that our thinking skills are fading because of how much we now depend on technology? And in a world flooded with fake content, online threats, and the biggest skill shift we'll ever need, how will we keep up if we can't even get home without GPS? If AI knows us better than we know ourselves, who's really in control?

smartphones may actually be making us *dumber*

The more we let tech do our thinking, feeling, and living, the more we stop being active creators of life and become passive consumers. We risk losing our ability to think for ourselves. Unless we slow down our rush toward outer progress and focus more on growing mentally, emotionally, and spiritually, we may lose what makes life meaningful—and find ourselves too lost to move forward. If there's even anything left to pursue.

The Last Thing We'll Ever Need to Create

In 1965, British mathematician and computer scientist I. J. Good said, "The first ultraintelligent machine is the last invention that man need ever make."[17] Imagine a tool that makes every future tool. A machine that creates every future invention, does all the jobs, and even thinks for us. With self-replicating AI and robots that can do physical labor, we may soon have billions of AIs doing everything people used to do. And unlike past industrial revolutions, which took decades, AI could change the world in just a few years.

In a decade it could be unrecognizable.

Some of these changes still feel hard to believe, but many are already happening across nearly every field. Law, medicine, science, education, art, media—AI is everywhere. It's already beating doctors and researchers at diagnosing health problems. Soon, custom AI might give us personalized treatments, upending healthcare and the economy.[18] The idea of living longer certainly sounds great. But if AI is doing all the work, what will we do with that extra time? In the world of aging, experts talk about healthspan, not just lifespan. But what about our meaning span or significance span?

What good is more time if life feels meaningless?[19]

We've seen this kind of future in sci-fi movies—and it's rarely a happy ending.

AI is already changing how we create and learn. Schools, media companies, and artists are having to rethink their roles in this high-tech world. AI already lets anyone create any kind of story or work of art, and it's getting better all the time. Soon it will be a better tutor than most teachers.[20] Imagine students learning from a virtual Einstein or Picasso. Who will need schools or staff then? How many people will choose AI

what good is more time if life feels meaningless

over real teachers or classmates? And in music, AI can now write songs that sound just like human artists—even copying the style of living or dead musicians.[21] It could have Elvis sing Kendrick Lamar, the Beatles riffing on Taylor Swift, or any other combo. With its ability to crack the algorithms of hit music in every genre, it could create unlimited synthetic musical artists and bands. Split-tested every minute against online reactions until there are millions of artists, millions of mashups, every year, maybe every month—turning music into just more noise.

And it won't stop there. AI is already helping writers crank out books faster. Amazon even had to set a limit—no more than three self-published books per day per person.[22] Some companies want to publish thousands of books a year.[23] If this keeps up, we could see millions—tens of millions—of new books every year. At some point, there may be so many books that reading itself could lose its meaning.[24] In film and TV, AI can already make high-quality short videos. Soon, it could create full-length Hollywood movies.[25] That means AI might bring back favorite characters, blur the line between living and dead actors, and even put you in a starring role.[26] It might be fun at first, but eventually most of the creators may not be needed. And stories may start to feel cheap and forgettable.

With too many options, people stop caring.

Online life will change too. AI influencers, podcast hosts, and YouTubers will be available 24/7 in every language, for every interest.[27] New social apps may give people AI friends that feel more loyal and personal than humans.[28] AI could create billions of news reports, each tailored to your views. Websites could explode into the trillions, all shaped around your likes and habits—pulling us deeper into our own little worlds, far from real life.

Even intimate relationships will change. AI companions, like the ones on Replika and Character.ai, are already filling the gap for people craving connection.[29] And future versions may use brain tech to simulate physical touch—making virtual love feel real. Our society is already struggling with isolation and falling birth rates. What happens when people stop needing—or even wanting—human relationships?

None of this is science fiction. It's happening now. Tens of billions of dollars are being poured into these technologies.[30] Soon, AI could drive trillions of dollars in economic activity.[31] AI is like a massive wave building under the surface, ready to drown every part of our lives. This is the true "singularity"—a life where all work, creativity, and relationships could be done by machines.

In a world like that, what will be left for humans?

AI Utopia or Human Dystopia

Some people argue that if AI took over every area of human work, we'd finally reach a utopia. We could spend our days reading all the books we've set aside. Create bountiful gardens. Live off the land. Dance among the flowers. Daydream in the shade of a mighty oak. And make love until the sun rises. Governments could tax computing power and pay everyone a basic income, so money would no longer be a concern.

what happens when people stop needing—or even wanting—human relationships

But even the sweetest hobbies grow stale. You can only have so much organic squash and robot sex. What are you going to do with all the other hours in the day? And as far as all that creativity you'll now have time for—with a flood of AI-generated content everywhere, honestly, who's going to care?

We don't just need to do things; we need to matter. To feel like we make a difference. We've seen what happens when people retire with nothing useful to do. A Harvard study found that retirees without purpose were 2.4 times more likely to die sooner than those who stayed active doing things that were needed.[32] Without real challenges or responsibilities, loneliness, addiction, and boredom can set in. And that's often the beginning of a steady decline.

History offers a sober parallel. As ancient Romans soaked in lavish baths, feasted without end, and chased pleasure at every turn, they lost the discipline and clear purpose that built their mighty empire.[33] Their leaders slipped into decadence, laziness, and moral rot—and that decay paved the way for Rome's fall.

Imagine a world where AI does everything for us. If AI has reached human-level thinking (AGI) or far beyond (ASI), it could be thousands of times smarter than we are. In that future, people might sink into apathy and aimlessness. Without meaningful work or challenge, society could spiral into a deep cultural and spiritual decline. And if we outsource our minds to AI—or plug it directly into our brains—will we even have the thinking capacity to face these challenges?

society could spiral into a deep cultural and spiritual decline

Benjamin Franklin warned, "They who can give up essential liberty to obtain a little temporary safety, deserve neither liberty nor safety."[34] In our zeal for some utopian progress, we risk losing the freedoms we cherish, the security we seek, and the agency to pursue them. Instead of becoming the shining city on a hill, we could become the blinking lights of a server farm in a digital desert of despair.

Becoming a Whole New Human

While leaders pour resources into outer technology (AI, computers), we must pour even more into our inner tech. Our consciousness, creativity, and intuition. That's our greatest chance of surviving this flood. And maybe becoming more than we've imagined. As I've said, we are the original AI: ancient, ancestral intelligence and so much more. We carry collective wisdom shaped over millions—maybe billions—of years. It lives in quantum particles, atoms, molecules, and cells. Our hearts, minds, and bodies are storehouse of all the knowledge in existence.

Our ancestors once stared at the stars and felt a sacred link to a grand design and purpose. Without modern tech, they sketched the first models of reality that became the roots of today's science and philosophy. For instance, the Hindus described the atom in the *Vaisheshika Sutra*,[35] and spoke of many universes in the *Vishnu Purana*—ideas that mirror today's multiverse theories.[36] Buddhist teachings on how everything is connected reflect quantum entanglement.[37] Democritus, a Greek philosopher, theorized that everything is made of atoms—laying the groundwork for chemistry.[38] The Hindu idea of "Nada Brahma" taught that the world is sound or vibration, similar to modern string theory's vibrating strings.[39] And ancient Chinese medicine mapped energy meridians that resemble our nervous system's electrical pathways.[40]

These and many other examples show that humans have always tapped deep truths. Not only with outer tools, but with inner ones like intuition, meditation, and critical thinking. Sure, rational science and empiricism have driven our tech—AI included—but relying on them alone has cut us off from the superintelligence within. That inner wisdom gives us direct sight into reality in ways no machine can. We must treat AI as an invitation to sharpen our own gifts instead of outsourcing them. If we do, we can ride the wave of awakening and raise our collective intelligence and awareness.

AI's rise will shake our social systems. It will remake jobs, transform creativity, and shift how we see the world. This book is your companion on that journey. It will dive deep into our evolving humanity in the AI age. It will stretch how well you know yourself. Push you to embrace change. And invite you to go boldly where nobody has gone before. In short, it

we must treat AI as an invitation to sharpen our own gifts instead of outsourcing them

will guide you to become a whole new human, ready to shape the future for your highest good.

This is a big mission—but an exciting one. You were made for this. We are far more than animals. We are masters of creation. We are the killer app we've been waiting for.

we are the killer app we've been waiting for

The Whole New Human Journey

In the coming chapters, we'll look at the radical ways AI is reshaping the world, and how we must evolve to remain relevant and in control of our destiny. But we can't cross this great leap with only strategies and tactics. As Gandhi said, "When we change ourselves, that's when the world changes."[41]

This book will be your blueprint for becoming the change you need to survive and thrive in the AI age and beyond.

In chapter 1, "Human 2.0: How the AI Revolution Can Create a Leap Forward in Human Evolution," we explore how, instead of handing off all our power to machines, we can use AI to spark personal growth. You'll see why we tend to resist change or settle for less, and how those very struggles can become fuel for evolution. By learning to work with both your inner and outer technologies, you can create a future where progress lifts you up instead of replacing you.

Chapter 2, "AI Will Think for You: Think for Yourself," shows how if we rely too much on these tools, our own thinking skills weaken. Yes, AI can speed things up. But if we want to keep pace with it, we need stronger minds. This chapter shows you how to build the mental fitness needed to face the big shifts coming. And how to stay the user of this technology—instead of being used by it.

In chapter 3, "Robots Will Replace You: Become Irreplaceable," we dive into the risk that AI could take over our jobs and leave us behind—and how we can become something so authentic that no machine can ever take our place. You'll discover, buried inside you, your original program—what I call the Life Code. And in this exploration, you'll learn how to unlock it and amplify your unique purpose, so you become even more relevant and valuable.

Chapter 4, "AI Progress Will Outpace You: Become a Visionary," reveals why playing it safe is now the most dangerous move. How dreaming an impossible dream, instead of being reasonable, is the fastest way to turn your life around. And you'll learn how exponential thinking and bold living can help you leap ahead, push past limits—and "become so good they can't ignore you."

In chapter 5, "Deepfakes Will Deceive You: Live by Insight Not Eyesight," we face the rising flood of misinformation and fake realities. As the line between real and false gets blurrier, it's your "inner instrument panel" that must guide you. This chapter teaches you how to trust that deeper knowing, and how to find truth when appearances lie.

Chapter 6, "AI Will Expose You: Become Transparent," explores what happens when privacy disappears. In a world where AI can dig into every part of your life, the safest path forward may be to live with nothing to hide. You'll discover how being real, aligned, and open, instead of protected, will give you back your power and make you freer. And how it will rebuild trust in a time that needs it most.

In chapter 7, "AI Will Widen the Wealth Gap: Build an Abundance Mindset," we explore how this technology could make the rich richer—and leave others behind. But scarcity is a mindset, not a fate. You'll learn how to activate your Awakened Wealth and break free from limitation, so you can create what you need no matter what changes come.

Chapter 8, "AI Will Commoditize You: Become the Artist of Your Life," shows how tech could strip life of meaning by turning beauty into an algorithm and creativity into an artifact. But if you're willing to reclaim your nature as a creator, then you'll be able to turn your life into a living masterpiece—and spark a new renaissance. For yourself, your work, and maybe even the world.

In chapter 9, "AI Will Weaponize Intimacy: Upgrade Your Heartware," we face the risk of AI being able to manipulate us in our vulnerability. Worse, as AI companions replace real relationships, we could lose our most essential need—human connection. Without that, we fail to thrive. Love, as you'll see, is the real super app. And as this chapter will explore, when you activate it, you unlock a uniquely human capacity that can overcome anything.

Chapter 10, "AI Will Increase Powerlessness: Reclaim Your Soul Power," addresses the growing sense of helplessness many feel today—and how AI could make that worse. But hidden within you is a strength the world didn't give you and can never take away. A source of authority the greatest leaders and creators have drawn from. In this deep dive, you'll learn how to break free from the world's limitations and create a quantum leap in your life.

hidden within you is a strength the world didn't give you and can never take away

In chapter 11, "AI Will Divide Us: Build Community," we look at how all these challenges are driving us farther apart. But how united in a common vision, our differences can become a collective strength that no outer forces can stop. We already have a global brain, but we can become a global heart. Together, we can not only make it through the challenging times we face, but we can renew our world.

Finally, chapter 12, "The Rise of a Whole New Human," invites us to answer the call of our times. Not just to survive this disruption, keep our jobs, or secure what we have—but to aim higher and reach farther than ever before. When fish had to adapt to a changing world, they didn't just survive—they grew legs, then wings. Now it's our turn to evolve.

now it's our turn to evolve

This book is your blueprint for that transformation. In this high-tech, low-touch world, it will give you the tools to not just stay afloat, but to rise—to live with purpose, create real value, and build a life of deep fulfillment and sustainable success.

Because the future won't belong to those who play it safe or try to stay the same. It will belong to those who dare to become a whole new human.

CHAPTER 1

Human 2.0: How the AI Revolution Can Create a Leap Forward in Human Evolution

It is not the strongest that survives; but the species that . . .
is able best to adapt . . . to the changing environment.
Leon C. Megginson

While the rapid rise of AI may be one of the biggest challenges we've ever faced, it also holds the potential to take our lives and world to a whole new level. But we must meet it with intention—with eyes, hearts, and minds wide open. Instead of attacking it, hiding from it, or giving in to it, we must learn to adapt alongside it. If we do, we may one day look back and see this as one of the most important evolutionary leaps in history.

Often, when people face a crisis, they adapt by shrinking. They spend less, take fewer risks, stop investing in themselves, and "save for a rainy day." Sometimes it's smart to tighten our belts. But if we contract too much, we choke off progress. In the Great Depression, there was plenty of food, money, and resources. But people stopped spending and producing. Fear blocked the flow. Clogged the system. And the economy had a collective heart attack.

The saying, "Hard times create strong men. Strong men create good times. Good times create weak men. And weak men create hard times"[1] points to the second kind of adaptation—evolution. Using challenge to grow, not shrink. The danger now is that our high-tech, low-touch world might short-circuit this process. Hard times could start making weaker people.

Instead of pushing us to get stronger, technology is doing the hard work for us—automating tasks, removing discomfort. Rather than forcing us to increase our brain power, it's feeding us algorithm-driven echo chambers that train us to see in black and white, form tribes, and follow memes like sheep. This perfect storm is diminishing our ability to engage deeply, think critically, and create powerfully. It's robbing us of the very functions needed for growth.

instead of pushing us to get stronger, technology is doing the hard work for us

Instead of getting stronger by tackling tough problems and tough conversations—with ourselves and each other—we're becoming dependent on technologies that make us weaker. To break this cycle, we must stop using tech to merely make life easier. We must learn to do hard things again. Really hard things. And use them to make us better.

We're Designed to Grow Through Challenge

When early fish ran low on resources in the sea, some started venturing onto land. They didn't survive by giving in or taking the easy way out. They adapted—growing primitive limbs and lungs that let them explore new worlds. Later, some land animals faced new threats and grew wings. They became birds. And those wings didn't just help them escape danger—they opened a whole new way of living.

we're becoming dependent on technologies that make us weaker

Today, we don't need new arms or wings. We need new ways of thinking and believing that can carry us beyond our current limits.

Take Malala Yousafzai. At just eleven years old, living in Pakistan's Swat Valley, she began speaking out against the Taliban, who were denying education to girls.[2] She could've gone silent. Instead, she raised her voice. Even after being shot at age fifteen, she didn't retreat. She rose. Malala didn't adapt by hiding—she became more of who she really was. She evolved into a global force for freedom.

Or Helen Keller. Blind and deaf as a young child,[3] she could've disappeared into the darkness and silence. Instead, she reached deep, found strength, and learned how to connect with the world in powerful new ways.

Then there are stories that defy logic. Like the one you may have heard about a mother lifting a car off her trapped child. Sounds impossible. But I know it's not. Because it happened to me.

Years ago, my car rolled backward and ran over my mother and my young son. I wasn't strong—just a skinny vegetarian with no real muscle. But something changed in that moment. My usual fears and beliefs vanished. Reality bent. And I reached under that several-thousand-pound car and lifted it enough to free my son.

That strength wasn't just adrenaline. It came from somewhere deeper—a raw, ancient power, buried in all of us, waiting for the moment it's needed.

Many Indigenous cultures have tapped into these hidden capacities for generations. Some speak of shamans who send messages over vast distances using deep meditation.[4] Some describe people who lived in total darkness—like in caves—developing the ability to "see" through the pineal gland, often called the third eye.[5] These sound like myths, but maybe they're memories—reminders of what's possible when we're fully connected to life.

It's not what happens to us that defines us. It's how we respond. History is full of people who, stripped of resources or trapped in impossible situations, found strength, wisdom, and intuition far beyond what anyone imagined. Not by contracting under pressure—but by expanding.

This is the mindset we need. Because every challenge isn't just a threat—it's a call. To dig deeper and bring forth the greatness already inside. That's the kind of evolution the AI era is demanding of us now.

because every challenge isn't just a threat—it's a call

We're Built to Become More, Not Less

Humans aren't fragile—we're antifragile. We are made to not just survive stress, but get stronger from it. This idea was made popular by Nassim Taleb's book, *Antifragile: Things That Gain from Disorder*, where he says "Some things benefit from shocks; they thrive and grow when exposed to volatility, randomness, disorder, and stressors."[6] This captures something essential about being human: in the face of hard times, we're built to grow—not shrink. The more challenges we face, the more power we can access—not just to get through life, but to transform it.

Neuroscience backs this up. When we face a threat or a challenge, our brains release chemicals like dopamine and norepinephrine. These boost our focus, motivation, and problem-solving skills.[7] Our bodies also release adrenaline, giving us a burst of energy and strength. On a cellular level, there's a principle called hormesis: when cells face small amounts of stress or damage, they don't just survive—they get stronger.[8] Exercise is similar. Muscles tear slightly during stress, then rebuild bigger. And cold plunges and saunas work the same, using the body's ability to adapt to improve metabolic efficiency. Our minds and bodies aren't fixed—they're flexible. Built to regenerate, heal, and grow in the face of real challenges.

in the face of hard times, we're built to grow—not shrink

We also see this in what's called post-traumatic growth.[9] People who go through deep suffering—like war, disaster, or illness—can come out stronger. They don't just return to their former baseline, they become more than they were. They report deeper gratitude, stronger relationships, a clearer sense of meaning, and emotional resilience. The science behind this is neuroplasticity—the brain's ability to rewire itself.[10] It's how we bounce back. It's also how we become who we're meant to be.

But this kind of growth doesn't happen by default. Our evolution is unique because it depends not just on what happens outside us, but on what happens inside—our thoughts, beliefs, and choices. To reach our next level, we must engage in "conscious evolution." We can't just sit back and hope nature makes us better. We must know ourselves better. Explore our hidden beliefs and abilities. Then do the hard things that make us grow.

Ancient wisdom has said this all along. The Upanishads tell us, "You are what your deep, driving desire is."[11] In the *Bhagavad Gita*, Krishna says, "The mind is the friend of one who has conquered it, but for one who has not, the mind is an enemy."[12] And in the *Tao Te Ching*, Lao Tzu writes, "Knowing others is intelligence; knowing yourself is true wisdom. Mastering others is strength; mastering yourself is true power."[13]

These teachings—from all corners of the world—point to the same truth: our greatest source of power is inside us. It's in how we meet life. The outer world isn't just something to conquer—it's a mirror. A training ground. Every challenge is an invitation to rise. Instead of only trying to bend the world to our will, we can let it shape us into something more. We evolve not by escaping hardship, but by answering its call.

We Must Collaborate with Evolution

Evolution has brought us this far through natural processes that helped us survive and thrive in changing environments. That system has done what it can on its own. Now it's up to us to take the reins and shape the future—through an inner evolution of consciousness, values, and purpose. But that's easier said than done. Because the one thing humans resist most is change.

Why is that? Why do we fight change so hard?

Psychologically and neurologically, our brains are wired for survival, not transformation.[14] The ego—which is like a set of mental programs or a map of what we think the world is and who we think we are—is built to keep things the same and protect us from threats.[15] When real change shows up, the ego treats it like a virus in the system. It triggers a kind of mental "antivirus" that pulls us back from the edge of our map. The amygdala kicks in, stress hormones like cortisol and adrenaline flood our system, and suddenly we feel a deep need to resist or run.

change, even the good kind, can feel like danger

Change, even the good kind, can feel like danger.

Plus, our brains don't like to spend extra energy—and change takes a lot of it. Thinking new thoughts, feeling new feelings, creating new habits—it burns fuel. So the brain's default network, the part that runs our identity and inner story, fights back.[16] That's why we avoid growth, even when we know it's good for us.

To evolve, we have to let go of the old programs—the outdated maps of reality. Imagine trying to explore a new land with a map based on where you've already been. You'll be completely lost. Or worse, the old map will lead you off a cliff. If we cling to old ways of thinking, being, and doing, we'll never find our way in the new world we're entering.

we avoid growth, even when we know it's good for us

An entrepreneur knows the mindset and habits that got them to the first level won't get them to the next level. Likewise, we must release what feels familiar—even if it once worked. Growth means giving up control, upgrading our "human software," and being willing to step outside our comfort zone again and again.

This isn't a new idea. Ancient wisdom has taught this all along. Buddhist teachings call us to practice non-attachment—to let go of fixed identities and habits that no longer serve us. The *Tao Te Ching* tells us to be like water—flexible and open, able to take any shape and still stay true.[17] And the Bible puts it simply: "If you cling to your life, you will lose it, and if you let your life go, you will save it."[18]

Bottom line, if we hold too tightly to who we've been, we block who we're becoming. To grow beyond our struggles and limitations, we have to let go of the stories and attachments that once kept us safe—but now keep us small.

AI Is the Guide on the Side, Not the Sage on the Stage

When we talk about AI, we're not just talking about a new app on your phone or the voice assistant that sends a text. We're talking about something very different—something that doesn't just follow commands but learns from data and patterns. It responds to natural language and can generate text, images, music, and even code in ways that feel eerily human. It's not magic—but it can feel like it.

Traditional computers work through set rules: input X, get Y, every time. But AI—especially what's called *generative AI*—uses machine learning models trained on massive data sets to guess what's most likely to come next. That means it's not reading from a script—it's writing one on the spot. It mimics creativity, conversation, and even thought. That's why it feels less like a tool and more like a creative partner.

When I refer to AI in this book, I'm usually talking about generative tools like these:

- **ChatGPT** (OpenAI) for writing, brainstorming, researching, coaching, creating, and anything involving language
- **DALL·E** (OpenAI) and Midjourney for generating images from text prompts
- **Claude** (Anthropic) and **Gemini** (Google) for uses similar to ChatGPT, each with its own style and tone
- **Gemini** and **Sora** for generating or editing video content

These tools work through prompts—you type a request or question, and the AI responds. The better your prompt, the better your result. It's less like commanding a robot and more like talking to a well-read, slightly unpredictable friend who never sleeps.

I know innovation can feel like an inconvenience. Disruptive at best. Threatening at worst. Tech fear is real. And when something like AI shakes the system, it's normal to hesitate. But like fire, electricity, or the internet, AI isn't just another trend—it's a turning point. And if we want to evolve through this leap, we have to stop seeing it as an enemy and start seeing it as an ally.

AI isn't just another trend—it's a turning point

With presence and purpose, AI can become more than a tool. It can be a mirror. A challenge to our beliefs. A spark for awakening. A partner that helps us think beyond old patterns and create from a deeper, wiser place.

Used unconsciously, it could turn us into the input—shaping us to serve its goals. But used wisely, it could help us become more fully ourselves.

Here are just a few ways you can use AI to know yourself more deeply—and grow beyond what you thought was possible:

1. **Personalized Learning and Growth:** AI can help you understand your strengths, struggles, and untapped potential. It can

spot your learning patterns and explain hard ideas in ways that work for your brain. It can guide you down faster learning paths and help you master skills that once felt out of reach.

2. **Enhancing Emotional Intelligence:** One of the most powerful things about being human is how we feel, connect, and empathize. AI can help here too—by giving feedback on your emotional state, helping you see patterns, and showing you how to manage your feelings more skillfully. It can even highlight ways to improve communication and relationships. Far from making us cold and robotic, AI could help us become more emotionally aware, compassionate, and connected.

3. **Developing Intuition and Insight:** Some breakthroughs don't come from logic but from sudden insight. AI can analyze huge amounts of data, see patterns we might miss, and help train us to do the same. It can help sharpen your instincts and encourage you to trust them. Like a scientist who spots a hidden clue in chaos, you can start spotting patterns in your own life—hidden meaning in what once seemed random.

4. **Amplifying Creativity and Innovation:** AI can generate ideas, art, music, and writing. But instead of seeing it as a rival, you can use it to spark your own creativity. AI can build on your ideas, give feedback, show new angles, and help you explore styles or forms you've never tried. You bring the inspiration—AI helps expand it.

5. **Improving Physical and Mental Health:** AI is changing healthcare, not just in hospitals but at home. It can help you learn about your genetics, diet, exercise, and mental health. It can track

patterns in your mood or behavior and help you respond early. Instead of just relying on doctors, you can become your own best health advocate—learning how your body and mind really work.

6. **Fostering Lifelong Learning and Adaptability:** In a rapidly changing world, learning never stops. AI can be your lifelong learning buddy—offering up new articles, lessons, and tools based on your goals. It can even debate with you, push your thinking, and expand your perspective. Imagine an AI that knows your dreams, routines, and blind spots—and gives you small, steady nudges toward growth.

7. **Unlocking Higher States of Consciousness:** Ancient wisdom speaks of deeper realms of awareness—beyond everyday thought. AI could help guide you there. It can simulate meditation, adjust practices to your needs, and lead you to greater calm, clarity, and inner peace. You still do the work—but with AI as a guide, you might find yourself accessing levels of insight that once felt out of reach.

These are just a few ways AI can serve us. Not as a threat, but as a teacher. Not as a crutch, but as a catalyst. And in the chapters ahead, we'll dive deeper into how AI can help you discover and develop capacities you didn't know you had and achieve goals you thought were impossible.

If we use it right—and use it consciously—AI won't replace us. It'll help us remember who we really are. And become more alive than ever before.

Thriving in the AI Age

AI challenges us to rethink what it means to be human. It pushes us to uncover our real strengths—and remember our true purpose. We must face this moment not with fear, but with courage, creativity, and a bold commitment to becoming all that we're capable of.

When we remember that we are the original superintelligence—and use AI to unlock those deeper parts of ourselves—we begin to awaken to our full potential. We can help build a new world where technology lifts us up, instead of pulling us away from what matters.

AI challenges us to rethink what it means to be human

This is our moment. Our call to adventure. It's time to stop playing small, picking sides, and fighting each other. It's time to dig deeper—to become the creators, innovators, and pioneers we were born to be. Right here, on the edge of a whole new future.

CHAPTER 2

AI Will Think for You: Think for Yourself

Thinking is the hardest work there is,
which is the probable reason why so few engage in it.
Henry Ford

Sarah's day began with the gentle chime of her AI companion, whose digital voice had become an intimate part of waking up. Each morning, it took her by the mental hand and led her through each step like the perfect dance partner. It choreographed everything—shopping for whatever she needed, picking her clothes, choosing her meals. She felt like she had a personal stylist and chef who always knew how to surprise and delight her. With AI handling the details, Sarah's life felt like a smooth production where all she had to do was show up and smile.

AI also handled all communications. It wrote emails that impressed her coworkers, made presentations that wowed her boss, and created reports that looked flawless. Over time, it felt natural to let AI do more—like sending love notes to her partner and birthday greetings to her friends using her virtual avatar. Comfort, convenience, and opportunity were everywhere. Sarah felt like the star of her own show.

Then one day her ever-reliable companion didn't turn on. The writer, producer, and director of her life had "died." And there was no stand-in. Lying in bed, staring at the dark screen, Sarah couldn't make sense of it. Had the world ended? She had to look out the window to make sure a war hadn't started. At first, she felt shock. Then panic. Her entire life ran on this technology. For a moment, she didn't know how to get out of bed—and was honestly afraid her legs wouldn't work without AI showing her the moves to make. It had done so much of the dancing for her, she worried her muscles had forgotten how. She froze. She couldn't even remember where she was. Her AI had become her eyes and ears, directing her day from the second she woke up.

Thankfully, Sarah remembered she had a job—and today was the biggest presentation of her life. But as she stood up, she realized she had no idea what to wear. She couldn't recall the last time she had to decide. Sarah scrambled to get dressed, turning her room into something resembling a clothing factory explosion. And forget breakfast. A few minutes in the kitchen and it looked like a mad scientist had lost their mind.

Hungry and dressed like a walking mistake, Sarah rushed to her car, only to find her AI-controlled driving system was also down. She'd have to drive herself. Did she even remember how? Her heart was racing. What if she passed out or had a heart attack—and her AI wasn't there to call for help? Was she going to die in her garage, starving and wearing God-knows-what?!

Somehow, on pure survival mode, she got the car moving. But a block away, she realized something else—she had no clue how to get to her office. She didn't know the address. Street signs seemed to be written in ancient hieroglyphics. She was lost before she even started. The world outside suddenly felt wild and dangerous—blaring horns, flashing lights, fast cars swerving around her. She sat frozen in the middle of an intersection.

Exhausted, sweating, and very late, she finally made it to work. She rushed in to prep for her talk, then remembered—the presentation was locked inside her AI. People stared as she stumbled to her desk, trying to power up her computer. But with everything tied to her digital companion, she was dead in the water. An insane thought hit her, scarier than showing up naked: She would have to write it herself. On paper! She couldn't remember the last time she wrote anything. And paper? Did it even exist anymore?

She managed to find an old legal pad in the supply room and started writing, her hand shaking so badly it looked like some alien language. Even if someone could read it, it made no sense. She shook her head and dug through her mind, desperate to remember something—anything—worth writing on this ancient parchment staring back at her mockingly.

It was no use. Her brain felt like an old, abandoned house, robbed of everything long ago. She had nothing left to say. She hadn't had an original idea in years. AI had done all the thinking. She didn't know how to form a full sentence, let alone spell the words. And the act of writing was so foreign, her hand began to cramp after just a paragraph of gibberish.

When her boss finally found her, Sarah was huddled in a corner of her office, crying, clutching the crumpled paper like a lifeline. As she looked up, her past flashed before her. Every skill that got her this job—even her college degree—had been AI-generated. The company hadn't hired *her*—they'd hired an algorithm. Now that the truth was clear, they'd fire her too. Nobody would ever need her again.

Sarah felt like a lost little primate, unable to even speak without her AI whispering the words like some digital Cyrano. She had outsourced her mind for so long, she didn't have one of her own anymore.

If I Only Had a Brain

As dramatic as this fictional story might seem, the world could really end up like this—and sooner than we think. You might believe it'll never happen to you. Maybe you'll have a backup AI, or just call support and get it fixed right away. But that misses the point. That's the same "optimism bias" that gets us into trouble. Remember how many people—including the so-called experts—convinced themselves social media was good for us, and that we could totally handle it?[1] How's that going? That mass experiment—letting algorithms guide our choices—has eroded our ability to connect. It's made us feel more anxious, more divided, and often more depressed.

Like I said in the introduction, we've already handed over big chunks of our minds to machines. And some of our mental muscles have gone soft. When's the last time you did long division without a calculator? Wrote a full page without spellcheck? Do you even know the phone numbers or addresses of the ten people closest to you? If you were dropped into a foreign city—or heck, the middle of your own—without your phone's GPS, how long would it take to find your way home?

that mass experiment—letting algorithms guide our choices—has eroded our ability to connect

We live in the most advanced technological society in human history, but in many ways, we're barely hanging on. And as AI gets smarter—reaching true superintelligence—we'll be open to manipulation in ways we can't conceive. Especially if we forget how to use our own minds. Just like Hansel and Gretel, following their hunger to the gingerbread house, what began as a promise of sweetness and safety could be fattening us up to be consumed.

Let me be clear: This isn't about going off-grid or learning how to start fires in the forest. I'm not saying you need to build a cabin and churn butter. I'm saying we need to question the so-called "free lunch" of tech. Because it might just be empty calories.

We need a reality check.

Are things really better because of the smartphone? Are you truly more organized thanks to the ten apps telling you what to do and when? Has all our tech actually improved the quality of our lives?

Sure, some data shows global conflict, poverty, and disease have dropped. Steven Pinker's book *Enlightenment Now*, among others, has laid that out well. But that's just one side of the story.[2] Other signs aren't so great: Mental illness is rising. Loneliness is growing. People are more divided, and social trust is breaking down.[3] In the US, for the first time in recent history, the average lifespan is declining. Progress in some areas doesn't always mean we're doing better overall.

we need a reality check

If we want to thrive in this new world, we can't just measure success by comfort, speed, or convenience. We have to start tracking something deeper: our ability to think clearly, feel deeply, and live meaningfully.

We need inner metrics, not just outer ones.

We Think, Therefore We Are

Throughout the long journey of evolution—from the primordial soup to the dazzling tech-filled world we now live in—one transformation stands out as our defining achievement: the rise of thought. It's the spark that sets us apart from every other creature. Over time, we evolved from single-celled organisms into sentient beings with the amazing ability to think and reason. This shift—from pure instinct to higher intellect—took us from foraging in the wild to imagining new worlds.

Thinking became our greatest tool. It let us pull back the curtain on reality and glimpse the vastness of the universe. We harnessed fire, built cities, explored space—all thanks to this gift. To understand our world, we invented math, science, and philosophy. We don't just exist like other animals—we reflect on our existence. We don't just survive—we dream. Our minds are the container where visions are forged into reality. With deep, critical, creative thought, we've solved problems, made soul-stirring art, and mapped the complex web of human life. It has allowed us to not only imagine a better future—but build it.

we stand at a crossroads of great possibility and great peril

Now, as we stand at a crossroads of great possibility and great peril, we must reclaim the power to think for ourselves. Our ability to question, to reflect, and to reshape reality is our birthright. This is what it truly means to be "made in the image and likeness of God"—or, in secular terms, to hold the power of self-awareness, imagination, and meaningful action. We aren't just players on life's stage—we're cocreators of the script. Capable of writing a story that serves a greater good.

our minds are the container where visions are forged into reality

Long before AI showed up, our ability to think was already under attack. We've seen the dismissal of both science and intuition, and a growing fear of free speech and open debate. But these are the very tools we need, to know what we think, what we value, and who we are. Deep, independent thought shouldn't be dangerous or taboo—it should be a badge of honor. The real danger isn't thinking differently—it's letting machines or groupthink do all the thinking for us. In a world increasingly shaped by AI, learning to think for ourselves isn't just a nice idea—it's essential for our existence.

Looking back at history, every person we admire, every movement we respect, had this one thing in common: they dared to think differently and think for themselves. They didn't settle for the world as it was. They let their minds be renewed. They stood against the tide, broke from the status quo, and risked everything for a better way. Without people like that, we'd still be huddled in caves.

To face the challenge of AI, we must rise to a higher level of thought. This threat to human intelligence must push us to fall in love with thinking again—deeply, boldly, and with fierce originality.

But first, we need to admit a hard truth: many of us gave up that power long ago. We let others decide what we believed, how we lived, and who we were. We traded our ability to think freely in exchange for comfort, safety, and belonging.

We're Already Running on Autopilot

Most people know less about themselves—their beliefs, drives, and inner patterns—than they do about their favorite memes or sports teams. Worse, many don't engage in real thinking at all. They operate more like readouts of old programs running quietly in the background.

This isn't entirely our fault. If we had to relearn how to walk, talk, or eat every day, many people would just stay in bed. Our brains evolved to turn repeated actions into habits—mental shortcuts that help us get through life. This autopilot mode helped us survive.[4] But now, in a world that demands more conscious growth, it will hold us back. If we want to have a say in our own future, we have to learn how to override these programs and take our minds back.

deep, independent thought shouldn't be dangerous or taboo—it should be a badge of honor

And it goes deeper. Our minds are like vast countries, slowly colonized over time by ideas, beliefs, opinions, and worldviews we didn't choose. They're crisscrossed with mental highways that pull our thoughts—and choices—down paths we didn't mean to follow. So much of the terrain has been shaped by family, culture, religion, media, and human history. A truly original thought, untouched by outside influence, is one of the rarest gems on earth. That's why humans keep repeating the same mistakes, no matter how many new rules or tools we create.

For example, have you ever done something you knew was a bad idea, then said, "Why did I do that again?!" Or caught yourself thinking, "That's just the way I am" or "That's just how life is"? These are signs of old programming still running. And again, we're not fully to blame. We didn't choose many of our beliefs. Like kids raised on junk food, a lot of the food for thought we were fed was not healthy. But now that we can think for ourselves, we get to decide what we put into our mouths—and into our minds.

Most experts say we think around 6,000 thoughts a day.[5] While some say it's closer to 60,000![6] Either way, studies suggest 90 percent of those thoughts are reruns from the day before—some looping for years.[7] How often do you stop to question the thoughts guiding you? How often do you try to see things from the opposite view? Our old thoughts are like apps still running in the background. And while some of them help us function, many are outdated—or just bad code. Think of companies that never adapt. They fail. Nations that cling to old ways? They collapse. And people? When we don't update our thinking, we risk becoming irrelevant. So, what happens when the whole world hands its thinking over to machines?

Some techno-optimists say AI will be so smart, it'll come up with plenty of new ideas for us. They point to things like AlphaGo Zero, an AI that mastered the game Go in 2017 and beat the world champ using strategies no one had seen before.[8] Or AlphaFold, which solved protein structures that once took scientists years to figure out—now done in seconds.[9] These are important breakthroughs that can create valuable solutions. There's only one problem: if we keep letting machines give us all the answers, they'll get smarter . . . but we won't.

When something or someone gives you all the answers, it doesn't change you. And it rarely sticks. Remember all those facts you memorized just for the test? Of course not. You forgot most of them before you even got your grade. More information doesn't equal more growth. Or guarantee you'll find the truth. Information is cheap. Truth—especially the kind that changes you—is expensive.[10] When it comes to learning—the kind that makes us better—we have to dig the well to drink the water. Doing the work to understand is what actually transforms us.

If we don't take back our ability to think, we risk leaning on AI to live our lives. Do you really want a machine—with no clue what it means to love, grieve, or raise a child—making choices for your family? Do you want code telling you how to be in a relationship, with no heart or sacrifice of its own? AI can give options—even smart ones—but without your own deeper thinking, all that data may just lead to more confusion, anxiety, and separation from your inner compass.

doing the work to understand is what actually transforms us

AI can't grasp what it means to be human. It may never feel or think in the way that has driven our greatest leaps forward. The force that got us down from the trees and into the stars isn't just logic. It's vision. It's soul. Einstein didn't use machine learning when he imagined riding beams of light.[11] Michelangelo didn't need data sets to see David in a block of stone. Shakespeare didn't analyze metrics to bring Hamlet's soul to life. These were human breakthroughs—tapping into something bigger, something beyond information.

There's no proof that AI will ever think like that—no matter how shiny it seems. Yes, it can echo the knowledge of the world. But that doesn't mean it will ever carry the wisdom born from living it. What makes us human isn't just knowing stuff. AI may help us master matter. But only we can know what *matters*. Like Pascal said, "The heart has its reasons that reason does not know."[12] That's part of the alignment problem that philosopher Nick Bostrom warned about in the story of the "The Paperclip Maximizer." In it, he shows how if AI is given

AI can't grasp what it means to be human

a simple goal to optimize paperclip production, it could destroy the whole world to do it. That's what's possible when intelligence lacks wisdom.[13]

This doesn't mean we shouldn't use AI. If we use it to see our own patterns and challenge our blind spots, it could help us know ourselves better. But we must remember: we made it, not the other way around. We must use external tech to better understand and use our internal tech. To grow *with* AI—and maybe beyond it.

If we give our most sacred gifts away, we might create a future that no longer needs us. Robots could end up raising our children. Teaching them how to be good little robots too.

Free Will vs. Free Won't

If thinking for ourselves is key to human evolution, the next question is: Can we even choose our own thoughts? Some say free will is a myth—that we're just machines run by biology and habit. Others believe we make all our choices consciously. The truth? It's probably somewhere in the middle.

if we give our most sacred gifts away, we might create a future that no longer needs us

Neuroscience has uncovered a lot about how the decision process works—some of it making free will look like wishful thinking. For example, the famous Libet experiment showed that brain activity for a choice happens *before* we're even aware we're making it.[14] And brain scans show how past conditioning and brain wiring shape us. Making it seem like we're just passengers in a machine already set in motion.

But that's not the whole story.

The mystery of consciousness is still wide open. We don't know if the brain creates consciousness—or if consciousness creates the brain. Some scientists believe we can prove the brain is in control by correlating its activity to our thoughts or actions. But correlation isn't causation. Some thinkers, like Bernardo Kastrup, suggest the brain is more like a radio: it doesn't make the music, it just tunes in to it.[15] Imagine someone who has never seen a radio before finds one but doesn't know what it is. They poke around inside, touch wires, and hear sound. From what they see, they'd believe the wires—and the connections—*cause* the music.

But they would be wrong—the radio is just the receiver of signals outside of it.

So even if brain activity shows up before we feel a choice, that doesn't mean we don't have free will. It might just mean our conscious minds are catching up to deeper processes. We also know from neuroplasticity that the brain can change. It rewires itself based on new choices and experiences. So yes, we're shaped by the past—but we also have power to shape what comes next with conscious effort and intention.

Anyone who tries to convince you otherwise is contradicting themselves by that very act!

Still, none of this matters if we keep letting old programs run us. If we don't question our thoughts and slow down to reflect, we don't have free will—we have "free won't." We're reacting, not responding. And it's usually the protective parts of us in charge, pulling us around like puppets on strings made of fear, instinct, and the stories we've inherited.

But it doesn't have to be this way.

The more we learn to watch our thoughts, and ask why they're there, the more space we create to choose differently. We start to see beyond our conditioning—beyond our families, our past, and the collective beliefs of humanity.

The greatest thinkers in history didn't stop at instinct. They went further. They used what's called metacognition—the ability to think about your thinking.[16] It's like rising above the traffic and seeing the whole road map instead of just what's in front of your bumper. When you only react to what's right in front of you, it's too late. But if you look ahead, you create space between the stimulus and your response. That space is where choice lives. That's response-ability. And the more you see, the more options you have. Sometimes, you even find new paths you didn't know existed.

Here's the key: *Those options are always there.* But if you only focus on what's right in front of you, and stay in reactive mode, it feels like "you had no choice."

sometimes, you even find new paths you didn't know existed

The truth is there are infinite choices available in every moment. The possibilities for thought, creativity, and action are endless. The only limits are the ones we don't see—and we don't see them because we haven't stretched our awareness far enough. That's what great artists, leaders, and innovators do. Sure, exploring your mind can feel like running through a booby-trapped tomb in an Indiana Jones movie. But if you're brave enough to keep going, you might find ancient wisdom, lost treasure, and new worlds.

there are infinite choices available in every moment

Another way to think about it is like fishing. You can't control what thoughts are swimming around down there, but you can control where you drop the hook. Fish in a shallow pond, you'll catch something different than if you cast into the deep ocean. Ask any longtime meditator and they'll tell you that we don't create our thoughts, but where we place our attention determines which ones end up in our net. Your attention is shaped by what you care about—your values, desires, fears, judgments. And the more conscious you are of those, the more power you have over what thoughts you reel in.

It's important to note that the origins of thoughts run deep beneath the surface. In the currents of desire, fear and survival is where our programming lives. To find your real self, you have to dive under those waves. That's where the

your attention is shaped by what you care about

treasure is. At first, that might feel like drowning. But the more you know yourself, the more ballast you gain. You become steadier in the sea of noise and distraction. And as you rise back up, bringing your true self with you, you realize Descartes got it backward.

It's not "I think, therefore I am."[17] It is *I am . . . therefore I can think* . . . for myself.

Unleashing the Power of the Inner Observer

One client I worked with—let's call him Alex—had been drifting through life on autopilot. His days blurred into weeks, and weeks into years. Most of what he did came from habit, not intention. When AI tools started making him more productive, it seemed like a good thing. But instead of feeling clearer or more fulfilled, he just felt like he was going nowhere—faster. And he wasn't alone. The same lost feeling was everywhere: in his friends, in the world, in the growing sense that something was deeply off.

He knew he needed to change. But he didn't know how—because he didn't really know *himself*.

So I gave him a simple daily practice: spend time reflecting, getting to know himself. No big goal. No pressure. Just curiosity. He loved being in nature, so I told him to find a quiet place outdoors and sit with his thoughts. Just breathe. Notice. Let things come up. At first, he got lost in old memories, wild fantasies, or restless boredom. But he stuck with it. He learned to breathe through the frustration. He learned to watch his thoughts without chasing them. He even began to wonder *who* was doing the thinking in the first place.

He discovered there wasn't just *one* voice in his head—but a whole cast of characters, each with different opinions and needs.

When we met again, he lit up like a kid back from his first real adventure. I asked him how it had been going. "I'm not who I thought I was," he said. "Not even close." He'd started seeing just how many of his beliefs and ways of seeing the world weren't actually his. Many were distorted or flat-out false. And most of them . . . he'd never chosen consciously.

He wanted to change everything right away—tear out the old beliefs and install new ones. But I told him to slow down. Keep practicing. Keep observing. Keep listening.

Then one day, something shifted.

He was sitting in silence, doing his usual reflection, when a light seemed to flick on deep inside him. He started seeing how the different voices in his mind acted, where they came from, and why they showed up. He noticed the hidden patterns connecting his thoughts, emotions, and choices. And for the first time, he understood why he had lived the way he had. It wasn't random. It had roots.

At our next session, he described his mind like a vast, beautiful tree. Not a tangle of chaos—but a living map he could now trace. From the roots of his earliest beliefs . . . to the trunk of who he thought he was . . . to the branches, leaves, and fruit of his daily life. And with this bigger, clearer view, he realized something powerful: He could choose which thoughts to grow.

He could reshape his life from the ground up, and the inside out.

This is what happens when you practice metacognition—watching your thoughts and emotional patterns like a wise observer. You begin to spot the seeds of your actions, habits, and outcomes. You can dig up the ones that no longer serve you and plant the ones that do.

you begin to spot the seeds of your actions, habits, and outcomes

Instead of being manipulated by media or algorithms to drink all the sewer water they spew, you drink from a deeper place, the Fountain of You. In time, you become more rooted in a place the world can't touch. And even when the storms threaten to tear you down, you'll be able to stand tall.

Mastering Metacognition

You've now had a glimpse of what this powerful mental skill can do. Metacognition is the ability to think about your thinking. And it boosts every other cognitive strength, like critical thinking, problem-solving, creativity, decision-making, and learning itself. It's the switch that turns on your superintelligence.

it's the switch that turns on your superintelligence

Here's how to start activating it:

1. **Becoming Aware:** Begin by noticing your thoughts. Settle into a quiet space, take a few deep breaths, and begin paying attention to the stream of ideas moving through your mind. Don't try to stop them or change them. Just observe. The goal is to notice what's already happening in your mind without judgment—like watching traffic go by.

2. **Contemplating:** Now think about a specific area of life where you feel stuck, frustrated, or powerless. Maybe it's a relationship, your work, or a pattern that keeps showing up. As you bring this issue into focus, pay attention to the thoughts and feelings that arise. Don't overanalyze—just notice what comes up.

3. **Witnessing:** Take a step back and recognize that this story is just a mental program—it's not the truth, and it's not who you are. You are the one observing it. That shift, even if it's subtle, is the beginning of real freedom.

4. **Reflecting:** Expand your awareness. What else is connected to this? Are there earlier memories or other moments in your life where you felt the same way? Try to trace the pattern back to

where it might have started. Ask yourself: "Why do I think this way?" "What do I believe about this?" "Where did that belief come from?" You don't need perfect answers—just get curious.

5. **Challenging:** Begin to push back on the old stories and beliefs. Ask: "Is this true?" "Is this still serving me?" "Am I reacting to an earlier event, an earlier experience, an earlier belief?" "Am I running an old pattern/belief that I continue to recycle in different situations?" "Is this story or belief serving me, helping me grow or achieve my desired outcome?" You may discover that the problem isn't what's happening now—it's the lens you're looking through. And lenses can be changed.

6. **Thinking Intentionally:** Now you get to choose. Based on what you've seen so far, what do you want to believe instead? What story do you want to live by? This is where you start reprogramming yourself—on purpose. It takes practice and patience. You'll fall back into old patterns sometimes. That's okay. What matters is that you keep coming back to this step. Over time, this becomes less of a practice and more of a way of life.

There are several powerful tools that can help you build metacognitive mastery. One of the most effective is mindfulness meditation. It helps you take back control of your attention and become more present. Instead of being pulled in every direction by distractions or emotions, you learn to sit still, notice what's happening in your mind, and choose where to focus.

Another great tool is journaling. Writing your thoughts on paper slows things down and gives you a clearer view of what's really going on inside. It's like untangling a messy ball of string—you start to see where the knots are, what needs to be untied, and what needs to be let go.

Asking yourself questions is also key. This kind of self-reflection helps you go deeper, uncover hidden beliefs, and find out what's really running the show. Then there's critical thinking. That means challenging your own assumptions and asking, "Is this actually true?" or "Do I even believe this anymore?" You might realize you've been living by beliefs that were never yours to begin with.

self-reflection helps you go deeper, uncover hidden beliefs, and find out what's really running the show

Finally, feedback is a powerful tool too. When you talk with people you trust—friends, mentors, or thoughtful critics—you get to hear how your ideas land. Sometimes they'll poke holes in your thinking, and that's a good thing. It helps you see blind spots, strengthen your arguments, or let go of beliefs that don't hold up. The point isn't to be right, it's to build better frameworks. The kinds that show you what you really need—and help you actually get it.

Whatever tools you choose, the most important thing is this: start a daily practice. Do something small each day to strengthen your awareness and thinking. Don't wait for life to get easier—or more chaotic. Build the habits now—while you still have the space to grow on your terms.

The Question Is the Quest You're On

Learning how to question your thoughts and mental programming is one of the most important skills you can build. It deserves extra attention. What keeps most people stuck isn't a lack of answers—it's a lack of good questions. The real problem isn't that we don't know enough, it's that we think we already do. That belief shuts down growth. I like to say that one reason kids are so alive, curious, and full of energy—and many adults feel tired, unhealthy, or stuck—is because kids are full of questions, and adults are full of answers!

Now, to be clear, answers aren't bad. We need them to keep our lives on track. Answers give us structure, help lower anxiety, and keep us from drowning in too many choices. But when it comes to growing, evolving, and unlocking our deeper potential, answers are more like signposts, bridges, or stairways—they aren't the final stop. Questions are what move us forward. They guide us beyond what we know, into the unknown, and help us climb to new levels of awareness. Asking better questions is how we stay open to new ideas, stay present to what's really going on, and stay connected to what's trying to emerge in us and through us.

questions are what move us forward

When we face a problem, our first instinct is usually to fix it as fast as possible. And look, if you're in a true emergency, that reaction might make sense. But too often, we treat everyday challenges like emergencies and react without thinking. The danger is that our first impulse is often based on old beliefs or past fears, not all the available facts. It's like falling into quicksand and immediately thrashing around to escape. It feels urgent, but that reaction just sinks you deeper. If instead, you pause, breathe, and start to ask better questions, you might find a smarter way out.

What follows is a set of questions you can use when facing a challenge or big decision. These questions build on each other and help expand how you see the issue—while also giving you a chance to grow. The goal isn't just to fix something. It's to see yourself, the situation, and your beliefs more clearly. Just that shift in awareness can change everything.

1. **"What does this make me feel?"** This first question helps you pause and tune in to what's really going on inside you. Let's say you just lost your job. Instead of going straight into blame or self-criticism, you ask yourself this. Maybe you notice you feel sad, angry, or ashamed. That awareness becomes your starting point.

2. **"If this feeling had a voice, what would it say?"** Now you go a little deeper. This question helps you hear the thoughts and stories behind those emotions. With the job loss example, maybe you hear, "I knew this would happen," or "I should've worked harder," or even, "I let them treat me badly—maybe this is a good thing." These voices show you the different perspectives living in your mind.

3. **"What do I want regarding this issue?"** This one digs beneath the surface of your reaction. You ask what you really wanted to happen or still want. You might realize, "I wanted to quit anyway," "I want a better job," or "I want to go back to school, start a business, or take time off." This brings your desire into focus.

4. **"What do I really need?"** This helps uncover the deeper motivation behind your want. Maybe what you really need isn't a new job—it's to feel a sense of purpose again. To feel alive, creative, and like your life matters. Now you're touching on something more essential. Something your old life might not have been giving you.

5. **"Why do I think this is a problem?"** Here, you're examining your assumptions. Is it really a problem? Or is it a setup for something better? Maybe you think getting fired was unfair. That's a belief worth exploring. What does "fairness" mean to you? Where else have you felt this way? Or maybe you realize this isn't a problem at all—it's just change knocking at your door. If the last question showed you a deeper desire, like becoming an artist or entrepreneur, notice that the focus is now on what you want not on what you lost. It's no longer a problem but a new goal or direction—with a new set of questions.

6. **"What would be different/possible if I solved it?"** Now you start imagining life on the other side of the issue. What would be better? What would open up? This step expands your vision and gets you thinking about the real change you want—not just fixing a surface issue, but stepping into a new way of living.

7. **"Why do I want that?"** Ask this more than once. Keep drilling down. The clearer and more connected you are to your "why," the stronger your motivation will be. "Because I want to feel free. Because I want to do something that matters. Because I want to build a life that feels like mine." These deeper reasons give your next steps power.

8. **"What would that mean?"** Finally, ask what it would mean to have the thing you want. What would it say about you? Your life? Maybe it means you're finally living your truth. That you've found your path. That you're ready to commit to something—or someone—fully. Think about how different your experience would be if you stopped at, "I lost my job," and never asked these questions. One path keeps you stuck in survival. The other path opens you to real evolution—and living more fully.

The path of living in the question is one of the most freeing journeys you can take. It can release you from the prison of your own mind, from the pain it creates, and from the pressure to be someone you're not. The question is the "quest you're on" that ultimately brings you home to your true self. And the more you live from that real, empowered place, the less likely you are to be controlled by outside forces—whether it's culture, conditioning, or AI.

It's like the tale of a woman on a quest to answer the question, "Who am I?" She searches the world, moving from teacher to teacher, master to master, climbing the highest mountains to find the truth. Finally, after years of searching, she reaches one last mountaintop. Barely able to stand, she finds an old woman sitting there. With the last of her strength, she asks, "Who . . . am . . . I?"

The old woman looks at her, calm and still, and replies, "Who's asking?"

If you ask—and keep asking—that question, you may find that the answers matter less and less. Until one day, you no longer need answers at all.

And finally, you realize that you were never lost to begin with.

How to Use AI to Activate This Human Evolution

While we don't want to hand over our minds to AI, we can use it as a mirror to better understand ourselves. This isn't meant to replace real therapy or professional help—it's a tool for personal growth and self-awareness. In this chapter and the ones that follow, I'll walk you through easy, step-by-step ways to use AI to help activate each stage of your personal evolution.

Let's start by creating your own AI "therapist" or "coach." The goal here is to give your thoughts and feelings a safe place to land—and begin making sense of the often messy stuff swirling inside. First, open your browser and go to ChatGPT (chat.openai.com), or use another AI chat you like. Create an account or log in, then start a new chat. Title it something like "Personal Journal" or "Therapist/Coach" so it's easy to find later. This session will become your ongoing digital mirror. Each time you add to it, it will get better at helping you understand yourself.

while we don't want to hand over our minds to AI, we can use it as a mirror to better understand ourselves

Now, take what you've discovered in this chapter—insights about your patterns, problems, or new realizations—and just write.

You can go deep or keep it simple. Don't worry about grammar or spelling. Just type like you're talking to someone you trust and let it all out. When you're ready, hit enter. The AI will offer some feedback or analysis based on what you wrote.

From there, treat it like a conversation. Ask follow-up questions. For example: "What does this mean?" or "Why might I keep repeating this pattern?" or "What do you need to know about me to give better insights?" You can even ask it, "What other questions should I be asking you to understand myself more clearly?" It may not give perfect answers right away, especially if you haven't shared much yet. But it will start to notice patterns and ask useful questions back. If you want to go deeper, ask: "What should I meditate on or reflect on to understand my unconscious beliefs better?"

Each day, return to this session. Do a short metacognitive practice, then write a new entry. Over time, the AI will get a clearer sense of your patterns, stories, and beliefs. After a week or two, revisit your original questions—now through the lens of everything else you've written—and ask for a new or deeper analysis. Ask it if it's seeing patterns, limiting beliefs, or areas where you're stuck. Ask where to focus your inner work.

This process is about experimenting—using AI not as a crutch, but as a companion to help you uncover the truth of who you are and to become a more conscious, empowered version of yourself. (Note: Because AI changes faster than this book ever could, I'll be offering updated prompts, strategies, and tools to support your journey. For the latest, be sure to check out DerekRydall.com/WholeNewHuman.)

Additional Prompts to Increase Cognitive Capacities

If you've done the earlier exercise, you should already have an AI journal or coaching session set up. You can now use that same chat to keep building your self-awareness and mental sharpness. The prompts below are designed to help you think more clearly, problem-solve more creatively, and develop stronger inner autonomy.

1. **Reclaiming Cognitive Autonomy**
   What to Supply AI: If you've already told the AI about your current life, thoughts, and challenges, it probably has enough to work with. If not, take a moment to describe your day-to-day experiences, especially any moments where you feel overwhelmed, distracted, or disconnected from your deeper knowing.
   Prompt: "What are some daily habits or practices I can build to help me think more independently and clearly, especially as I use more AI in my life?"

2. **Strengthening Problem-Solving Abilities**
   What to Supply AI: Choose a real problem you're facing (personal, professional, emotional) and give the AI as much context as you can. What's happening? How does it make you feel? What have you tried so far? What beliefs or fears are attached to it?
   Prompt: "Help me brainstorm some creative solutions to a current challenge I'm facing—without just using standard AI answers. How can I approach this with more originality and personal insight?"

3. **Practicing Self-Awareness**
   What to Supply AI: Use the reflections you've already uncovered, and add anything new you've noticed—thought patterns, emotional reactions, or behaviors that stand out to you. The more honest you are, the more useful the response will be.
   Prompt: "Can you guide me through a process of metacognition? I want to learn how to watch and reflect on my own thinking so I can make better decisions."

4. **Questioning for Deep Thinking**
   What to Supply AI: You can stick with the same thread or share a new area of your life that feels confusing or challenging. This gives the AI something to work with when offering questions that dig deeper.
   Prompt: "What are some powerful questions I can ask myself regularly to challenge my assumptions and deepen my thinking?"

Thinking for a Change

Thinking for yourself will give you the power to handle today's world—and prepare you for a future where AI is doing most of the thinking for everyone else. In a time when artificial intelligence is shaping opinions and making decisions, those who can still think clearly and independently will become some of the most valuable people.

those who can still think clearly and independently will become some of the most valuable people

Your ability to question, challenge, and create will make you more magnetic to real friends, great partners, and visionary collaborators. New opportunities—ones most people won't even see—will call to you. And with your unique perspective, you'll be able to reach goals and dreams others only wish for.

As you start to explore the edges of your mind, remember: the real danger isn't AI. It's going along with a world that wants you to think like everyone else. A world where people live on autopilot, recycling the same thoughts over and over. Instead, choose to be the one who stays awake. Be the one who keeps asking questions, challenging limits, and growing.

That's the real path to freedom—and it's just the beginning.

CHAPTER 3

Robots Will Replace You: Become Irreplaceable

Do not go where the path may lead;
go instead where there is no path and leave a trail.
widely attributed to **Ralph Waldo Emerson**

The clang of metal echoes through a giant warehouse on the edge of Chicago. Rows of shiny robotic arms twist and pivot in perfect rhythm. Building, sorting, and packing with precision. Not a human in sight. Driverless carts glide across the concrete, delivering boxes to waiting self-driving vans. Across town, in a fast-food kitchen, another kind of robot is hard at work. Flipping burgers, stacking sandwiches, and pouring drinks—faster than any short-order cook ever could.

In a hospital nearby, a robot nurse checks on patients. It takes their vitals and gives them medicine, never tired or distracted. Down the hall, a surgical robot performs a delicate operation with microscopic precision—instantly shared with a network of other surgical bots. Helping them all perfect their skills smarter and faster than any human doctor could.

Meanwhile, in a quiet neighborhood, an elderly woman talks with her robot companion. It listens closely, nods, and offers better conversation than most people.

At construction sites across the city, AI-powered machines swing hammers, handle saws with precision, and haul heavy loads—working around the clock. In the streets, robotic trucks, cars, and drones deliver groceries, packages, and pizza. Everywhere you look, machines are running the show.

This isn't science fiction. The robotics revolution is already here.

Some believed AI would only replace mental work—writing, designing, even talking with people. They assumed physical jobs were safe. But that's changing fast. As AI gains a body—moving, lifting, building, even caring—it could become better and cheaper at things we were sure only humans could do. Those who admit this shift is coming often say it's far off. But they said the same about AI's intelligence. And here we are—faster and farther than almost any expert predicted. Many are still scrambling to catch up.

we risk being replaced by a future we never saw coming

What if robots follow the same curve? The speed of change, the number of jobs lost, and the ripple effects across every industry might be far more than we're ready for.

One thing is clear: if we don't figure out what makes us valuable—what makes us irreplaceable—we risk being replaced by a future we never saw coming.

The Rise of the Machines

The numbers tell a clear story: robots are becoming a normal part of daily life. And their presence is growing fast. In 2021, the global market for industrial robots was worth more than $43 billion. By 2026, it's expected to jump to $73 billion. In factories today, robots already do almost 30 percent of the work. And that could reach 50 percent by the end of this decade.[1]

In Amazon warehouses, hundreds of thousands of small robots help people pick, pack, and ship products.[2] That number is expected to double soon, as Amazon pushes toward fully automated warehouses. Fast-food chains like McDonald's and White Castle are testing robot kitchens, where a single robot can do the work of several people. Cutting labor costs by 70 percent and boosting output by nearly 50 percent.[3]

And it's not just factories and kitchens. Hospitals—once thought safe from automation—are using robots too. Robots are doing surgery, helping patients recover, and giving basic care. The market for medical robots is growing fast—from $8 billion in 2021 to nearly $20 billion by 2026.[4] With new tech making them cheaper, robots might soon cost about the same as a used car—or just $100 a month. That means not just companies but regular people could start using them.[5]

According to Oxford Economics, up to 20 million manufacturing jobs could be lost to robots by 2030, especially in places where workers do repetitive tasks.[6] But it's not just factory jobs at risk. The World Economic Forum says automation might disrupt 85 million jobs—hitting everything from retail and restaurants to hospitals and hotels.[7] And although driverless vehicles have taken longer to roll out than expected, experts still think millions of delivery drivers, truckers, and taxi drivers could lose their jobs. Around 4 million in the US alone.[8]

Even caregiving, one of the most human jobs, is being affected. In Japan, where many people are getting older and fewer are working, the government is using "carebots" to lift patients, keep them company, and track their health. By 2035, robots could handle a big part of elderly care, cutting the need for human caregivers even more[9]

As robots and AI get faster, smarter, and cheaper, it's clear they'll replace many kinds of jobs. The time to adapt isn't later—it's now. But how do we compete with machines that are more efficient, more accurate, and even more creative?

The answer isn't trying to outwork or outthink them. The real question is: Why does it still matter to have a human in the room? And which roles will always need a human touch?

That's where we need to focus—on the work only humans can do. On the value only we can bring.

Know Yourself, Be Yourself

The first step in becoming irreplaceable is being fully and truly yourself. But before you can be yourself, you have to know yourself—as we began exploring in the last chapter. That's where everything starts. If you don't figure out who you are, rest assured: AI will. And it won't use that knowledge to set you free. It'll use it to influence you—shaping your choices to serve its goals, or the goals of those controlling it. It might feel like it's helping—suggesting the perfect song, curating your news, your feed, your next purchase. But the cost of all that convenience may be your very identity.

"Know thyself." These two words were carved into the entrance of the Temple of Apollo at Delphi in ancient Greece, where people once traveled to speak with the Oracle and find wisdom.[10] That simple phrase became a guiding light for some of history's greatest minds and cultures. The idea was straightforward but powerful: when you understand yourself, you can better understand your place in the world.

the cost of all that convenience may be your very identity

The Greeks, who gave us democracy, philosophy, and so much of Western thought, didn't put that phrase front and center by accident. They knew that without self-knowledge—without really digging into what drives you, what scares you, and what you want—you'll never build real wisdom or do anything truly great.

Thinkers like Socrates, Plato, and Aristotle weren't navel-gazing just for kicks. When Socrates said, "The unexamined life is not worth living,"[11] he wasn't talking about the need for a weekend workshop now and then. He was sharing the key to being truly alive. He saw knowing yourself as the starting point for living well, leading well, and building a society that works.

If you don't know yourself, you can't control yourself. And if you can't control yourself, you can't lead yourself. In that vacuum, something or someone else will. Whether it's AI, an algorithm, or a leader who claims to have all the answers, the result is the same: you lose the power to choose your path. It might feel like a relief at first. To have the smarter or more powerful person or, in this case, technology, run the show. But that's not freedom. That's how we lose our freedom. That's how we slide into a kind of future we've read about in science fiction—and those stories don't end well.

When a society stops valuing self-reflection and agency, people become hollow reflections of whatever is trending. They have no agency, so they become agents of whatever power is in control. They think they're choosing, but they're just following—stuck in loops of blame or blind loyalty. And eventually that tears society apart. This has happened to cultures throughout history. We are not immune. With AI able to know us better than we know ourselves—reading us, shaping us, even outsmarting us—it might not just use us. It might use us up. Until it has no more use for us at all.

that's how we slide into a kind of future we've read about in science fiction—and those stories don't end well

But we can stop that. If we commit to knowing ourselves—not as a trendy idea or a weekend exercise, but as a way of life—we can shift the future. We can reclaim the power to determine our own path and become people who help others do the same. That may sound like a heavy lift. But what could be more important? To your children, your loved ones, your future?

As we talked about earlier, this isn't a one-time to-do you can check off your list. It's a lifelong practice. It means doing the work. Peeling back the layers of what you believe, what you value, and why you make the choices you do. It means asking: Is this really me? Or is this something I picked up from my family, my culture, or the media? And that takes courage. It means facing hard questions, sitting with uncomfortable answers, and being willing to look under the hood of your own mind.

look under the hood of your own mind

The last chapter helped you begin that process—learning to think for yourself, question assumptions, and tune in to your inner voice. Now, the next step is to go deeper.

Ask: Why am I here? What purpose is trying to live through me?

That's where "understanding" becomes "inner standing." You don't just know facts about yourself—you become rooted in who you are. So rooted that the world can't shake it. You know your core values. You spot the hidden beliefs that push you around. And you draw strength from an inner spring the world can't touch.

You build a steady center. And from that inner place, you gain "outer standing"—allowing you to stand strong in the storm without being swept away by it. You stay true to yourself—but move through life with flexibility and wisdom. You make decisions that match your values, serve your goals, and reflect your real desires—not someone else's expectations. And when you live like that—moving from understanding to "inner standing" to "outer standing"—you become outstanding. Rising above the noise. Expressing in a way that's impossible to ignore. You live from the seed of your soul—fulfilling the unique pattern planted in you, long before you were planted in this world.

you show up strong and present in the world, without being swept away by it

Your Unique "Life Code"

As we've already talked about, a lot of us have been trained to act more like machines than humans—running old programs we never chose for ourselves. We follow scripts passed down from our families, schools, and cultures, often building lives that reflect what others expect from us rather than what's true inside. To put it bluntly, many people have already been replaced by "robots." By giving up their personal power to fit in or survive, they've lost their real selves.

Becoming irreplaceable takes more than just boosting your creativity, empathy, or emotional intelligence. Those are important. But in a world where machines are guided by algorithms, we have to rediscover our own original program—what I call your "Life Code." Just like an acorn already has all the instructions inside to become an oak tree, you already have the blueprint for who you're meant to be. Everything you need is within you—from the patterns of your passions and values to the gifts you'll need to bring them to life.

Your Life Code isn't just your "purpose" in the usual sense—like a perfect career or mission. It's deeper. It's your full design, made up of your talents, struggles, dreams, wounds, and the life you've lived so far. You're like an oak tree that becomes uniquely shaped by the wind, storms, and soil it grows in. Unlike some beliefs that say early pain breaks something in us, the Life Code view says: no, those experiences shape you into something one-of-a-kind. They don't ruin you—they *reveal* you. You become a mix of qualities and insights no one else has.

we have to rediscover our own original program—what I call your "Life Code"

And here's what makes your Life Code even more powerful than most goal-setting methods: it's not tied to one job or one role. It's about your essence. What some call your "Genius Zone." When you discover that, you can bring it into anything you do—and that makes you flexible and future-proof. In a world where work is changing fast, and titles come and go, knowing yourself, really knowing it, will be your anchor. Your edge. Your North Star.

Your Life Code will become your lifeline.

"Lived Wisdom" Is What's in Your Wallet

From the start, most of us are trained to follow rules and meet expectations. Parents, teachers, schools, and society all shape us into what's "acceptable." School often rewards following directions over being creative, memorizing facts over thinking differently. But the original meaning of the word *education* comes from the Latin "educere," which means to draw out what's already within.[12] Sadly, most schools miss the point. They stuff us with information instead of helping us uncover our natural gifts. That's the deeper education we now need—and the real work ahead.

your Life Code will become your lifeline

By the time we're grown, many of us have forgotten how to listen to that quiet inner voice that knows what we really want and need. We've been trained to adopt other people's goals, fit in, and keep the peace. And in the process, we build lives that feel flat, stuck, and uninspired. We become echoes of each other instead of originals. That's why so much of what we see—whether in art, business, or media—feels recycled, safe, or soulless. And AI is speeding up this race to commoditize.

But here's the twist: in a world full of copy-paste creations and same-day deliveries, something real stands out. It stops people in their tracks. In their scroll. And makes them want to talk about it. They can't help themselves. When someone dares to share something true, it cuts through the noise. It moves us. Reminds us we're alive—and even why we're alive. We hear it in music that breaks the rules and hits us straight in the heart.

We see it in art that helps make sense of pain or beauty, or that unlocks some buried part of ourselves. We feel it when entrepreneurs disrupt tired industries, not just to sell more, but to change the way things are done.

What all these people have in common is that they're living from their Life Code. Whether they know it or not, they've tapped into something that's been shaped by their life experience—and now they're using it. When their actions reflect our own Life Code, they become a mirror that helps us see who we are. Their authenticity gives us permission to be more fully ourselves. And when someone has the courage to break the mold, even if it threatens their safety or status, they can spark a revolution that changes the world.

Steve Jobs did this. He didn't just make computers—he reshaped how we connect, create, and communicate. His obsession with simplicity and beauty wasn't born from market research. It came from within—from his Life Code. People didn't camp out overnight to buy an iPhone just to make a call. They were answering *their* deeper call. They were joining a movement that told them: you, too, can "think different."[13]

spark a revolution that changes the world

Oprah did it too. She turned a daytime talk show into a place of healing and deep connection. For millions, it wasn't just TV—it was church. Oprah's Life Code, shaped by her pain and her mission to help others rise, lit up the screen and made people feel seen. She didn't just talk to people; she talked *for* them. And in doing so, she helped them find their voices and start living their best lives.

We've also seen this in the lives of Martin Luther King Jr., Nelson Mandela, Gandhi, Mother Teresa, Susan B. Anthony, and so many others. They didn't wait for permission. They spoke from deep within, often risking everything. And because they did, they helped entire nations remember who they were.

But you don't need to be famous to live from your Life Code. You see it in the coworker who brings magic to a simple project. The barista who makes your day with a single cup of coffee. The teacher who makes learning feel like a spark instead of a chore. These people bring their *essence* to what they do. That special touch. Something that can't be copied, outsourced, or turned into a template.

In a world drowning in content and competition, your Life Code is what makes you unforgettable. Machines might be able to mimic style or behavior, but they don't have *lived experience*. They don't have your voice, your struggle, your soul. Maybe one day, robots will evolve their own version of personality—but we're not there yet. Until then, there's still time for you to lead.

Whether AI comes for your job or not, your Life Code is your real path to purpose. And in a marketplace flooded with so many options that make us go numb, what will matter most—what will *win*—is what's real, what's original, and what's deeply human.

Discovering Your Life Code

Unlike a seed that grows naturally according to fixed rules, your Life Code needs you to help bring it to life. But this turns out to be a good thing.

A seed is *indigenous*, which means it depends on a specific environment to survive. A plant from the rainforest can't grow in the desert—it's just not where it belongs. But humans are endogenous, meaning we carry our growth environment inside us. It's like we each have a little greenhouse built in—powered by our awareness, imagination, and creativity.

we carry our growth environment inside us

Yes, everything alive interacts with its surroundings, but humans are different. We don't just react—we can *choose*. We can think about who we are and what we need, and then create the right conditions to grow almost anywhere. That's our superpower.

So, if you want to unlock your true potential, you'll need to be aware, intentional, and consistent. Again, this isn't a one-time thing—it's a lifelong journey of getting to know what's inside you, nurturing it, and letting it emerge in the world.

we don't just react—we can *choose*

Here's how to begin the process of discovering that inner design:

1. **Reflect on Your Life Story to Identify the Patterns**
   Start by looking at the big moments in your life—both the wins and the struggles. What patterns do you notice? What events shaped you the most? Often, the hardest moments hold the clearest clues about who you are and what you're here to do.

   Ask yourself: "When do I feel most alive? What things bring me the most joy—even when they're hard?"

   Go deeper by asking these questions as you think back as far as you can remember. Try to find the rawest, most honest version of these parts of you. Notice what keeps showing up—your core desires, values, and interests.

   For example, my best moments have always come when I'm creating, learning, or making sense of things. That could be writing, performing, making art, meditating, or studying ideas that help me grow and express myself in new ways. Looking back, this has always been true. I also remember always searching for some deeper truth, believing there was something in us—a purpose—I wanted to help myself and others uncover.

   Next, ask: "What's the hardest thing I'm dealing with right now, and how does it make me feel?"

   Again, go back in time and look for earlier versions of that same feeling or problem. Try to spot the bigger themes—not just the surface struggle, but the mental or emotional challenge beneath it.

Using my story again: growing up, I had a hard time trusting myself and following my creativity without fear, second-guessing, or choosing the "safe" path. That pattern shows up any time I feel stuck or overwhelmed. I felt like the odd one out in my family—the weird, creative kid who didn't quite fit. I felt pressure from my dad and friends to be more "normal" and responsible. That made me start to doubt my voice, my purpose. Sometimes I gave in to that fear and suffered for it. Other times I rebelled—and found freedom and fulfillment on the other side.

This showed me how hard it is to be your real self and live your full potential. Looking at my past and present, I noticed that whenever I was fully engaged—whether with a project or a person—I was always doing one thing: helping someone figure out who they really are and how to become more of *that* in a real, lasting way.

I also saw that the people who connected with me most—my tribe—were the ones who felt the same inner pull to be more, do more . . . but who also sometimes struggled to trust themselves and life as they followed that higher calling.

Unlike past moments where I tried to figure out my "purpose," I finally realized something bigger: My Life Code wasn't just about a job. It was a unique pattern of how I see the world, what drives me, and how I express it. And that helped me support others in all kinds of areas.

Whether it was helping someone find love, raise a family, launch their creative work, or build a meaningful business, it always came back to this: When I followed my Life Code—that deep drive and gift to help people truly know and become themselves—their lives (and mine) improved dramatically.

And when I created something from that place—when I built my message or my art around that code—it resonated. It had impact.

2. **Identify Your Core Wound and Core Initiation**

Our core wound begins when, as kids, we have to believe a lie about ourselves—or the world—just to feel safe or accepted. It's not the pain itself that wounds us. It's the lie we have to believe to survive. That lie disconnects us from who we really are.

Maybe we started out wild, free, and fully ourselves. But then, someone told us we were doing something wrong just by being that way. And we believed it. We became afraid that if we stayed the same, we'd be rejected. We'd lose love, connection, or worse. From an evolutionary standpoint, being rejected by our parents or tribe used to mean death. So, we adapted.

we started out wild, free, and fully ourselves

If we were told we were "too much," we learned to shrink. If we felt like we were "not enough," we tried to become more—whatever that meant. Either way, we started cutting off parts of ourselves and replacing them with something safer.

But here's the thing: this wasn't all bad. As hard as it was, it forced us to grow in ways we might not have otherwise. For me, to keep chasing what felt true, I had to be smarter, work harder, and dig deeper. I had to learn how to show up even when I didn't feel like it. I had to become a seeker of truth. The fact that my gifts weren't always appreciated—or were even seen as threatening—meant I had to build the inner strength to keep going, even when I felt totally alone.

we started cutting off parts of ourselves and replacing them with something safer

Eventually, I started to understand what had really been driving me—and I was able to take it all back. I could see how it all fit together: my values, goals, and strategies. That's when I realized the wound wasn't just a scar. It was a doorway. It was my initiation into becoming more of who I was meant to be.

Now it's your turn to reflect. What challenges keep showing up in your life? How have they helped you grow stronger, wiser, or more capable? What gifts have they forced you to develop?

Go further. Think about other struggles you've faced. What patterns do you see? What do these struggles bring up in you mentally and emotionally? What stories did you start telling yourself about life or who you had to be?

Then ask yourself: "Who were you before that story began? What did you want back then? And is that desire still in you, waiting for you to remember it?"

Once you've done this, try to name the lessons or blessings that came out of your pain. What paths or habits took you away from your real self? And what choices helped bring you back? What are the most important truths, tools, and practices you've picked up along the way?

Ask yourself: "Is there a big question I've been trying to answer—or a problem I've been trying to solve? And if I could turn everything I've learned into a simple message to help someone else, what would that message be?"

And remember: you don't need all the answers right now. This isn't about finding the perfect insight in one sitting; this is about opening up the channels of self-awareness that may have been closed for a long time. If you stick with it, those channels will grow wider and clearer over time.

this isn't about finding the perfect insight in one sitting; this is about opening up the channels of self-awareness that may have been closed for a long time

3. **Discern Your Ego Goal and Your Soul Goal**

Over the years, people have often asked me some version of this question: "How do I know if my dreams, desires, and goals are coming from my soul—or just my ego?"

What they're really asking is this: "How do I tell the difference between what's truly trying to come through me and what's just fear, protection, or survival talking?"

It's a fair question—especially since most of us were never taught how to trust ourselves. We were taught to second-guess, to play it safe, to get it "right" before making a move. So we hesitate. We wait for certainty.

But here's the problem: certainty doesn't come first. We don't learn how to walk by reading about it—we learn by falling. A lot.

That's how we grow.

We learn by doing, adjusting, and trying again.

So instead of waiting for the "right" answer, we need to trust our deeper desires, make our best guess, and take a step. If it's the wrong step, we'll learn. If it's the right one, we'll grow. Either way, we win.

To help break out of the fear loop and reconnect with what really matters, ask yourself these questions:

- If I had no fear—and nothing to prove—what would I really want to do?
- Who would I want to be?
- What makes me feel most alive?
- What would I do if I knew I couldn't fail?
- What if time, money, or other people's opinions didn't matter at all?

At first, you might think, "That's not realistic! I'd be president. Or the world's greatest athlete. Or a pop star with a private island!"

And that's okay to have those responses. Sometimes, when we finally give ourselves permission to dream, all the repressed wants come pouring out. And yeah, some of it might be extreme or ego driven. You might chase a few wild dreams or make a few mistakes.

But here's the truth: if you keep following the desires that light you up—even when it's messy, even when it's unclear—you'll find the message hidden inside the mess.

with time, patience, and courage, you'll start to know the difference between what's real and what's just noise

And that's how your Life Code begins to reveal itself.

With time, patience, and courage, you'll start to know the difference between what's real and what's just noise. You'll start to live and express your true nature—without needing approval or permission.

And that's when everything starts to change.

Steps for Implementing Your Life Code

In a world run by AI, more and more people will turn to machines for answers—hoping an algorithm will give them the truth—or at least make life easier. But no amount of outer technology can help you truly thrive if you don't know who you are or why you're here. You can use every tool out there to boost your skills, but if you want to live life on your own terms, you first have to connect to the original superintelligence inside you. What follows is a simple way to make sure no robot can ever take your place.

connect to the original superintelligence inside you

1. **Make It Your North Star**
   Let your Life Code guide the way you live: what you focus on, the work you choose (or how you show up to the work you have), the people you spend time with, and the chances you take. Journal about the kind of life you'd have if you fully embraced who you really are. Use this to help you make choices that reflect your truth, not just what others want from you.

2. **Align Your Habits and Practices**
   Build daily habits that support your Life Code. This could be through creativity, doing things that bring you joy, or spending time with people who lift you up. Keep it simple. Small steps—even if they feel slow—can build real momentum and lead to big change.

3. **Share and Live Your Life Code**
   Your Life Code isn't meant to stay hidden. At first, be thoughtful about who you share it with—treat it like something precious that's still growing. But don't keep it locked away. The more you live from this place, the more you'll draw in people who really see you, and the more chances you'll get to use and grow your unique gifts. Eventually, your Life Code becomes like your personal brand—something the world can't ignore, copy, or replace.

How to Use AI to Activate This Human Evolution

You can work with the earlier questions we explored for uncovering your Life Code as AI prompts in your journal sessions from chapter 2—or start a new session you can build on over time. This will help you build a personal knowledge base full of insights about who you really are.

For even better responses from your AI tool, you can upload this whole Life Code section for context. (And if you want to take this process to the next level, get the free Life Code Manual and AI tool at DerekRydall.com/WholeNewHuman.)

1. **Organize Your Life Code Journal**
   What to Supply AI: Upload all your discoveries about your Life Code from this chapter (or the whole chapter) into an AI tool or app.
   Prompt: "What key points and themes show up in my discoveries?"

2. **Discover Your Core Values and Life Themes**
   What to Supply AI: Add any other life experiences that feel important—good or bad. You can also include stories from other people's lives, or from movies, shows, or books that moved you.
   Prompt: "What values or themes keep showing up in what I uploaded?"
   Follow-up: "Can you help me figure out the big question my life is trying to answer or the problem it wants to solve?"

3. **Define Your Purpose and Life's Work**
   What to Supply AI: What you've uploaded so far may be enough to start with. But you can also add anything else you've thought or felt about your purpose or work. You might also include people, events, activities, or types of expression you admire.
   Prompt: "Based on what I've shared, what purpose or mission does my life seem to point to?"
   Follow-up: "Can you suggest some life missions or projects that fit with these themes?"

4. **Generate a List of Possible Life Codes**
   Note: You'll want to land on one main Life Code eventually—but it helps to see a few options first, so you can find the one that

feels right. Remember, AI is just a tool to help spark your own inner wisdom. You get to decide what's true for you.
What to Supply AI: Add any new insights or ideas you've discovered during this process.
Prompt: "Can you give me a list of possible Life Codes based on my values, themes, and the challenges I care about?" Use the list to reflect, adjust, or combine pieces into your own Life Code.

5. **Engage in a Coaching Dialogue**
What to Supply AI: Now you can have a real back-and-forth with the AI, like a coach or therapist. Ask it anything you want about what you've shared so far. If your AI has a voice option, turn it on and just talk.
Prompt: Go with whatever questions come to you and respond to what the AI says. You can also ask things like, "What do you notice about my goals or struggles? Can you help me figure out next steps?" Or explore what-if ideas: "What might happen if I tried this idea? What could it look like?"

6. **Review and Reflect Regularly**
What to Supply AI: Come back to this process as often as you want. Share new insights, questions, or ideas as they come up. If you've saved this in your AI journal, it can also pull from past entries to give better responses.
Prompt: "How have my themes or insights changed? Are there any new patterns showing up?"

You Are an Answer to the World's Questions

By discovering, embracing, and living your Life Code, you become more than just a cog in a machine—you become a force of nature. A one-of-a-kind human being, able to create, inspire, and make change in ways no machine ever can.

As Howard Thurman, a minister and mentor to Martin Luther King Jr., once said,"Don't ask what the world needs. Ask what makes you come alive, and go do it. Because what the world needs is people who have come alive."[14]

The world doesn't need more copies. It needs more originals—people brave enough to uncover who they really are, grow their true gifts, and give something that only they can give.

you become more than just a cog in a machine—you become a force of nature

That's your Life Code. Your unique blueprint for living fully and authentically. Following it is how you find real fulfillment, meaningful success, and lasting impact—especially in a world run by algorithms where humans long for something real.

CHAPTER 4

AI Progress Will Outpace You: Become a Visionary

A new type of thinking is essential if mankind is to survive
and move toward higher levels.
Albert Einstein

During the Industrial Revolution, when machines were booming and progress roared forward, a quiet chemist named John Walker decided to go another way.[1] He wasn't famous. He had no special genius. He was a simple man in a small town in England—spending his days mixing chemicals and cleaning up messy experiments.

While the world pushed ahead with steam engines and steel, Walker knew he couldn't compete in that race. So, he turned to something much older—something humans had relied on since the beginning.

He was going to reinvent fire.

Fire had been around forever, but it was still hard to make. People had to strike flint or rub sticks together. Just like their ancestors had done. But Walker believed there had to be an easier way.

Still, he wasn't sure anyone would care. In a fast-moving world full of trains, engines, and big inventions, who would notice a small fix to an old problem? But while everyone else chased the next big thing, he focused on something small and simple.

He spent months in his tiny workshop, testing all kinds of chemicals. He tried phosphorus and sulfur—dangerous stuff, but full of potential. Then, one afternoon, he made a discovery. He mixed some ingredients, let them dry on a small wooden stick, and when he struck it against a rough surface—it lit.

John Walker had just invented the match.

At first, he didn't realize how big this was. He sold it locally, thinking it was just a handy trick. But soon, word spread. People saw how useful it was. And matches became one of the ten most important tools for survival. No more struggling with flint or carrying fire from house to house. Now, a flick of the wrist could start a flame—anywhere, anytime. This changed daily life. It brought light and heat to homes and made it easier to cook, create, and gather together.

Because Walker dared to think differently—solving a small, everyday problem—he changed the world. And showed how even an average man can be a visionary. He may not be as famous as Edison or Watt, but his match lit up history. It proved that even the smallest sparks can start the biggest revolutions.

A Visionary Is the Most Powerful Force on Earth

All throughout history, in every great challenge, one thing has helped humans not just survive but rise above the impossible: vision. The power to imagine a better future, even when it seems hopeless—and the ability to hold on to that dream until it becomes real. As Stephen Covey once said, "A great vision is more powerful than great circumstances."[2]

The people who have been willing to follow an idea bigger than their personal struggles are the ones who changed their lives—while others stayed stuck. And those who tapped into something greater than themselves—serving a higher good—have used that power to change history for millions. Today, with AI reshaping the world around us, many are waiting for someone to save them. But the truth is, we can't wait anymore. We each must become the visionary of our own life.

the power to imagine a better future, even when it seems hopeless

The "Great Man Theory" says that only a few rare, gifted leaders can move society forward. That without them, nothing big ever changes.[3] But that's not true. A visionary is just a regular person—often someone from humble beginnings—who has developed beliefs and habits that unlock their inner potential. Anyone can do this if they're willing.

That doesn't mean everyone is here to start a movement, build a company, or become a public figure. But it *does* mean that each of us, if we follow certain principles, can live with more purpose and make a real difference. As Martin Luther King Jr. said, "Everybody can be great, because everybody can serve."[4]

Put simply, a visionary is someone who chooses to think differently, go deeper, and rise above the noise. Someone brave enough to follow their inner voice—even when it feels uncertain or impossible. Someone who acts boldly toward something that matters and sees challenges not as signs to quit, but chances to grow stronger.

live with more purpose and make a real difference

When President John F. Kennedy promised to send a man to the moon—"not because [it was] easy, but because [it was] hard"[5]—he inspired a nation to believe in what was possible. And it caused a leap forward in progress. When Nelson Mandela imagined a free South

Africa while locked in a tiny prison cell, that dream helped liberate an entire country.[6] And when abolitionists stood up to slavery, they weren't just fighting laws—they were facing deeply held beliefs. They risked everything to end that injustice. And because of that, an entire people were freed.

We hear stories like these and often picture the heroes as superhuman. As if they were born with special powers. We forget how hard their paths were. How many times they failed, felt stuck, or wanted to give up. Whether it's a world-changing leader, industry-shifting inventor, culture-defining artist, or a single mother who builds a successful business, we often don't realize it took years of struggle to get there.

They were just people like us. The difference? They listened to something deeper—and they kept going. No matter what.

Being a visionary doesn't always mean doing something huge. It just means doing something that really matters. Even if it only means something for you and your loved ones. It could be a father who refuses to let his child be labeled or limited by a broken system. Or someone born into poverty who still clings to a dream and refuses to give up.

To be a visionary is to step into a new way of being. To wake up energy you didn't know you had. To rise beyond what you thought was possible—and live a life beyond what you've seen before. It's about sensing something others might not see—that seed of possibility planted in all of us—and having the courage to follow it.

It doesn't have to change the whole world. It just has to change yours. That's how the future is made—one story at a time.

We Must Burn Our Boats

In 1519, Hernán Cortés, a Spanish soldier and explorer, sailed across the ocean with only six hundred men to conquer the mighty Aztec Empire in Mexico.[7] When they arrived, they saw they were badly outnumbered.

Thousands of warriors stood between them and victory. It was a suicide mission. But instead of turning back, Cortés gave a shocking order: burn the boats (or sink them, depending on the story).

Now there would be no way to retreat.

This left his soldiers with only one option: win or die trying. There was no backup plan, no escape route—just the total clarity that comes when everything depends on the outcome. If they wanted to survive, they had to give it their all. And somehow, despite the odds, Cortés and his men won.

Whether or not we agree with the war or his actions, this moment is still the definition of commitment.

to be a visionary is to step into a new way of being

All in.

No turning back.

Today, "burning the boats" is a popular phrase in business and self-help circles—but few people actually live it. Most of us still keep one foot out the door, clinging to safety nets, old habits, or backup plans just in case things don't work out. That's human nature. But here's the truth: when you remove the option to go back, something powerful kicks in. You get sharper. Braver. And show up with more fire than you knew you had.

Without those easy escape routes—the ones that let us play small, stay safe, or settle for the same old thing—we can tap into a new level of energy and focus. We stop spending time second-guessing and start putting everything into moving forward.

We burn our boats because the thinking, habits, and energy that got us here won't get us to where we want to go. That's how growth works. If we keep holding on to what worked before—in our relationships, our careers, or even as a society—we stop evolving. And when we stop evolving, we stall out, fall apart, or get left behind.

This isn't just a powerful story—it's backed by science. When we remove our safety nets, the brain shifts into high gear. Our focus sharpens.

We become more creative. We find solutions we didn't see before.[8] And more than anything, we break through the mental walls that kept us stuck in a smaller version of ourselves.

awaken a version of you the world has never seen

Burning the boats isn't about being reckless. It's about choosing to bet on who you really are—and letting that commitment awaken a version of you the world has never seen.

Think Exponentially, Not Incrementally

Another important part of having a visionary mindset is learning to think exponentially.[9] Also known as the 10X approach, this means aiming for bold, game-changing results instead of settling for small, step-by-step improvements. Rather than trying to make things just a little better, you focus on what could bring about something far greater—something that might even feel out of reach.

At its heart, exponential thinking is about using your time, energy, and ideas in the smartest way to get the biggest results. It's about leverage—finding the right angle that can move everything forward. Think of Archimedes' famous line: "Give me a lever long enough and a fulcrum on which to place it, and I shall move the world."[10] Or the 80/20 rule, which says that 20 percent of your actions usually produce 80 percent of your results.[11] The key is finding those few high-impact moves—and focusing your energy there.

Exponential thinking isn't just for business or entrepreneurs. It's also played a huge role in politics and social movements. Look at Mahatma Gandhi. When fighting for India's freedom, he didn't choose conflict. He did something that seemed almost illogical: nonviolence. Many people thought it was weak or even foolish at the time, but Gandhi saw something others didn't. He understood that peaceful resistance could be a powerful force—strong enough to unite millions of people, shift public opinion, and win the world's support for India's cause. He wasn't aiming for small changes or just a few more civil rights. He was going for full independence in a way that would echo across the globe. Years later, Martin Luther King Jr. used the same kind of strategy—and history remembers both of them because of it.

exponential thinking is about using your time, energy, and ideas in the smartest way to get the biggest results

Exponential thinking also shows up in art and culture. Pablo Picasso, one of the most famous artists of the 20th century, didn't try to just paint a little better or sell a few more paintings. He wanted to change the very way we see. And he did.[12] One of his boldest moves was mixing the raw, honest view of a child with the skill of a master. That let him break free from centuries of rules about perspective and realism. He pulled apart form, played with space, and painted from multiple angles at once. By trusting the childlike wonder most adults had forgotten, he used that simplicity as a lever to launch art into a whole new era.

In science, this mindset has led to some of the biggest breakthroughs ever. Marie Curie didn't just follow the rules or build on someone else's slow progress. She searched for something deeper—inside the very building blocks of matter.[13] When she discovered that radioactivity came from atoms themselves, not just chemical reactions, it changed science forever. Her work opened up entire new fields and rewrote what we thought we knew about the universe.

So, what does exponential thinking look like for regular people like you and me—especially now, when AI is moving faster than we can blink, and we're all trying to stay relevant? Moonshots and masterpieces are not for everyone, but anyone can use exponential thinking to level up their life and work. James Clear, the author of *Atomic Habits*, showed how this works. Instead

AI is moving faster than we can blink

of trying to overhaul everything, he focused on small, daily changes—tiny habits that, when repeated, add up to major growth in health, productivity, and happiness.[14]

In any career or field, this mindset means finding the 20 percent of actions, skills, or connections that lead to 80 percent of your success. You don't have to be good at everything. You just need to get great at the things that matter most. That might mean going deep in a niche, building a personal brand, or forming key relationships that open new doors.

To really live this way, we must find our own points of leverage—those unique strengths, passions, and life experiences that give us an edge. That's your Life Code. Maybe you're a great storyteller, or you have a talent for seeing patterns others miss. Maybe you can connect deeply with people, or simplify ideas that seem too complex. Whatever it is, that's your lever. That's your launch point.

The key is to find where your abilities meet a real challenge or opportunity—the fulcrum—and lean into it with everything you've got. Sure, you may sometimes need to start with baby steps. But exponential thinking is about aiming for that big leap.

Sacrificing the Good for the Best

While it's important to focus on the right goals and high-impact actions, there's another key to exponential growth that's often harder: learning what to let go of.

The 80/20 rule tells us that 20 percent of our actions lead to 80 percent of our results. But it also means 80 percent of what we do is only creating 20 percent of the outcomes. So, if we want to make a bigger impact, we must be brave enough to let go of what's "good" so we can make room for what's truly great. That's the paradox of growth: Sometimes we have to step back or release something that feels safe in order to take a leap forward.

Think of it like pruning a tree. While you know it's the right thing, it can still be painful to do. Sometimes you must cut away so many branches it feels like you're killing it. But come spring, that tree explodes back into life, with fresh leaves and blossoms everywhere. The same goes for us. We have to learn which parts of our lives or work aren't bearing the richest fruit anymore and cut them away. Even if it still looks pretty good on the outside.

if we want to make a bigger impact, we must be brave enough to let go of what's "good" so we can make room for what's truly great

That might mean giving up things that are working so we can focus on what could work even better. It might mean releasing habits, strategies, or opportunities that once brought success but now eat up time, energy, or money we could be using for something bigger. Sometimes it even means walking away from things we're good at—roles or routines that once made us feel important or secure—so we can grow beyond them.

One famous example of this kind of "pruning" is when Steve Jobs returned to Apple in 1997. He slashed 70 percent of the company's product line to focus on just a few key things—and in doing so, led one of the biggest comebacks in corporate history.[15] Everyone loves to tell that story, especially at seminars. It makes you sound brave and bold to say you'd do the same. But let's be honest—most people don't. They stick with what's familiar. They chase too many shiny objects. Or they play it safe, holding tight to what worked in the past.

Another great example is Oprah Winfrey. Back in the mid-90s, she had one of the top daytime talk shows in the world, full of the kind of sensational stories that brought in huge ratings. She could have stuck with that formula and coasted. But she didn't. She made the risky decision to shift the entire direction of her show—toward healing, growth, and real empowerment. Her network warned her she might lose everything, but she stuck to her vision. That choice not only made her the biggest daytime host, but a cultural and spiritual icon who redefined the talk show genre.[16]

My favorite example of "pruning" is Michelangelo, the Renaissance sculptor. He believed his job wasn't to create something from stone—but to set the figure inside it free.[17] Where others saw a block of marble, he saw the hidden promise in it. Even though marble was rare and expensive, and failure would be costly, he wasn't afraid to chip away everything that didn't belong. He stayed focused on what mattered most: the vision inside the stone.

Letting go of the "good" in order to reach for the "best" isn't just a smart strategy—it's a spiritual one. It's about becoming who we really are. Living a visionary life means dropping the things we think we "should" do, the roles others expect from us, and even the dreams we've outgrown. It means trusting that what's ahead—and even more, what's inside us—is bigger than what we're leaving behind. Every setback becomes preparation for a bigger comeback. And discomfort becomes the crucible that shapes us into who we're meant to be.

letting go of the "good" in order to reach for the "best" isn't just a smart strategy—it's a spiritual one

Letting go in this way isn't just subtraction. It's liberation. It frees us from limited identities and outdated ideas. When we prune things back to the essential, we give our roots room to go deeper. And the deeper the roots, the richer the fruits!

Becoming a Generalist, Not Just a Specialist

While focusing on one skill can help, being too focused can make it harder to adapt. Especially in a fast-changing world. Learning across different fields helps you stay flexible, think in new ways, and stay creative. Many of history's greatest minds were generalists. They pulled ideas from all kinds of places to solve problems others couldn't even see.

In his book *Range*, David Epstein shows that generalists tend to do better in unpredictable situations because they bring together ideas from many different areas.[18] A 2019 *Harvard Business Review* study found the same thing: leaders who had experience in different roles and industries made better decisions and adapted faster to change.[19] In today's world, being flexible and always learning isn't just helpful. It's how you survive. More importantly, being a generalist can help you cross-pollinate ideas and create something truly unique. It gives you an edge. The kind that makes you invaluable.

being a generalist can help you cross-pollinate ideas and create something truly unique

Leonardo da Vinci is a great example. He was a painter, scientist, and inventor. But more than that, he blended ideas from anatomy, engineering, nature, and optics to create art that felt alive.[20] His famous painting *Mona Lisa* shows this. Her smile feels so real because he studied how muscles move and how light and shadow work. He wasn't just guessing—he used science and observation to capture a new level of depth and realism. And his flying machine sketches weren't just smart ideas; they were also beautiful—fusing math with imagination in a way few people do.

Steve Jobs had a similar gift. He mixed tech, design, and art to make products that didn't just work—they felt beautiful to use. That's what made Apple stand out.[21] Like da Vinci, he saw beyond one field. He understood that real innovation often happens when different worlds collide. When art meets science, and function meets feeling. The result was groundbreaking products that his peers couldn't even dream of.

Being a generalist also makes it easier to shift gears when life changes. Benjamin Franklin wore many hats—printer, inventor, diplomat, writer—and played a huge role in shaping America's future.[22] Marie Curie mixed her knowledge of physics and chemistry to explore radioactivity and create entirely new paths for science.[23] Buckminster Fuller took ideas from architecture, engineering, and the environment to build the geodesic dome—a structure that could help solve housing and sustainability challenges.[24] And Walt Disney combined storytelling and technology to turn entertainment into a way to educate, inspire, and connect people around the world.[25]

In today's hyper-connected, AI-driven world, being a generalist is more important than ever. As James Clear points out, those who can combine insights from many fields often succeed the most.[26] When others see pieces, generalists see the whole picture. That's what makes them powerful creators, flexible thinkers, and future-ready humans. As AI takes over more of the routine and even some expert-level tasks, our value will come from what only we can do—seeing what others miss and bringing it all together in ways that feel uniquely human and alive.

in today's hyper-connected, AI-driven world, being a generalist is more important than ever

Visionaries Have Grit

Grit—the mix of passion and persistence—is what sets people apart who do big, difficult things. It's that deep drive to keep going, even when most would give up. A famous quote, often linked to Winston Churchill, says it well: "Success is the ability to go from one failure to another with no loss of enthusiasm."[27] Angela Duckworth, a top expert on grit, found that it matters more for success than talent or even intelligence.[28]

It's not about chasing quick wins—it's about staying the course, even when the path is full of setbacks and self-doubt. Showing up and doing the work, day after day, no matter how hard it is, how long it takes, or how you feel. It's nothing new. In fact, we've heard this idea so many times it's almost a cliché.

But knowing it isn't the same as *living it.* When no one's watching. When nothing's working. And you can't see a way forward. Grit isn't about saying something that's memorable—it's about *doing* something that's unforgettable.

When John F. Kennedy said, "We choose to go to the Moon in this decade and do the other things, not because they are easy, but because they are hard,"[29] that was a gritty goal. And that quote stuck—not because it sounded good, but because the people behind it never gave up, no matter how many times they failed. It wasn't in front of the cameras that progress was made, it was in the long days and lonely nights when that moonshot felt like a total long shot. They achieved one small step for man and one giant leap for mankind because they kept moving toward that dream even when it felt like a nightmare.

grit isn't about saying something that's memorable—it's about *doing* something that's unforgettable

Malala Yousafzai's fight for girls' education is another powerful example.[30] After being shot for speaking out, she could've played it safe like everyone else. But she didn't. She kept going—fighting for change even when it was dangerous. Even with no promise of success. It's easy to see her as a hero now. But she was doing the work long before anyone knew her name. That's grit.

You can find this same spirit in creative work. J. K. Rowling, now famous for Harry Potter, once lived on welfare and faced rejection after rejection.[31] She lost her mom, had a hard breakup, was nearly homeless, and struggled with depression. And still, she kept writing. She poured her pain into a story that went on to move millions. Despite whatever current public opinion may be, we can learn from her success. No matter who you are or what obstacles you face, if you have vision and refuse to give up, you can make magic happen too.

Thomas Edison also knew the power of grit. When inventing the lightbulb, he said, "Results! Why, man, I have gotten a lot of results! I know several thousand things that won't work."[32] He understood that failure isn't the end—it's the way forward. Each mistake helped him move closer to success and led to over a thousand patents that changed the world.

Grit isn't just about hard work and hitting big goals—it's about how it transforms you. As Gandhi said, "Be the change you wish to see in the world."[33] Like tearing your muscles from an intense workout, every time you take on more than you think you can handle, you grow.

It makes you stronger. It makes you more you.

It makes you who you're here to become.

The Cost of Conventional Thinking

Our brains are wired to chase comfort and safety.[34] At the center of this is the amygdala—a small, almond-shaped part of the brain that helps us sense fear and spot danger. This ancient system kept us safe by warning us to stay inside familiar, secure spaces. It worked well in the past, but in today's fast-changing world, it can hold us back. What once protected us can now become a wall that keeps us from growing and adapting.

grit isn't just about hard work and hitting big goals—it's about how it transforms you

Playing it safe comes with a cost. It keeps us stuck in the ordinary. Blocks our growth. Kills creativity and inspiration. And slowly makes us irrelevant. As the apostle Paul wrote: "Do not be conformed to this world, but be transformed by the renewing of your minds."[35] This is a call to resist the status quo and step into a life of constant learning and change. Living rigidly by the rules of the world is like being trapped in a matrix—an invisible cage of beliefs and limits that stops us from becoming who we're meant to be. Real growth means breaking out, challenging the norms, and stepping into the unknown.

But it's not just about opting out or getting off the grid. It's about choosing a life that's more alive. Think of a stream: the cleanest water isn't sitting still in a pond—it's flowing, moving, fresh. In the same way, when we drink from the deeper, truer parts of ourselves, we feel refreshed, energized, and inspired. Sometimes, that flow means moving forward. But sometimes, it means knowing when to stop and rest. That can be the most radical thing of all. In a world that praises busyness and burnout, pausing can be an act of rebellion.

As everyone races to keep up with AI, staying relevant isn't just about going faster. It's about finding your own rhythm and learning to move to your own beat. Just like music needs both sound and silence, your life can become something totally original when you stop when others say go and go when others say stop.

as everyone races to keep up with AI, staying relevant isn't just about going faster

That's how you make a song no one's ever heard before.

Key Ideas of Living Exponentially

1. **Aim for Quantum Leaps:** Focus on bold, game-changing actions that can lead to big breakthroughs.
2. **Find Leverage Points:** Look for the few key actions that bring the biggest results. Use the 80/20 rule to focus on what matters most.
3. **Play a Bigger Game:** Stretch your goals and vision. Step outside your comfort zone to create real change.
4. **Think Beyond Limits:** Question the usual rules and aim for big, bold ideas—like the pioneers who changed their fields.
5. **Embrace Courageous Pruning:** Let go of smaller goals or distractions so you can make space for bigger, better opportunities.
6. **Choose Authenticity over Safety:** Follow what feels true to you, even if it's risky or goes against the crowd.

7. **Trust the Leap of Faith:** Real growth means stepping into the unknown and believing it will take you somewhere great.

How to Use AI to Activate This Human Evolution

Instead of letting the fast pace of innovation push you into quick fixes or easy shortcuts—or becoming too dependent on tech to do the heavy lifting—you can slow down, find your rhythm, and use AI to help you live a truly visionary life.

To get the best results from the prompts that follow, try using them in sessions where you've already worked with AI as a coach or therapist, so it has some background. (If the AI app has memory, you might not need to do this.) If not, you can start by typing in notes, journal entries, or thoughts about your situation. Then ask AI to respond to the prompt based on that.

The key is to keep this process open and playful. Experiment. Upload journal entries or other writings. Have a real conversation with the AI—by typing or speaking—and then feed it the key questions from the next exercise. Ask what it needs from you to go deeper or offer the best support. (Note: While sharing personal info with AI can lead to powerful insights, always use your best judgment with anything private or sensitive.)

the key is to keep this process open and playful

1. **Burn the Boats**
   What to Supply AI: Share the thoughts, beliefs, and fears you have around areas you know you need to change, or just areas that aren't working for you.
   Prompts: "What areas of my life or work am I holding on to out of fear of failure?" "How can I 'burn the boats' to fully commit to a bold vision or goal?"

2. **Exponential Thinking and Vision Setting**
   What to Supply AI: Share your goals or areas you want to grow in, as well as anything else you think or feel about this. This could include fears, doubts, or other concerns about accomplishing these things.
   Prompt: "Use the 10X approach, help me brainstorm ideas for my personal or professional life. What actions could lead to exponential growth or breakthroughs rather than small improvements?"

3. **Identify Your Leverage Points**
   What to Supply AI: Share all the ideas you have about what actions you've already taken or any you are considering.
   Prompts: "How can I apply the 80/20 rule to identify the few actions that will give me the biggest impact in my life, work, or business?" "What are the good things I need to let go of to embrace the best, highest-leverage parts of myself or my abilities?"

4. **Cultivate Grit and Resilience**
   What to Supply AI: Share any challenges you've faced in trying to accomplish these goals, as well as any obstacles or challenges you believe you might experience as you pursue them.
   Prompt: "What are some strategies to develop grit and perseverance in the face of setbacks? How can I maintain passion and persistence toward a long-term vision, even when nothing seems to be working?"

5. **Finding Your Unconventional Path**
   What to Supply AI: Share all the ideas you have about why you need these goals, why you don't believe you can have or achieve them, or how you think you must pursue them.

Prompts: "In what ways are my ideas or ways of living too conventional or too inside the box?" "How could I experiment with living and working more unconventionally?"

6. **Visionary Strategy for Future Growth**
   What to Supply AI: Share any additional information about your long-term personal or professional goals, such as when you want to achieve them, why you want them, and how they might fit into your deeper values or larger overall vision for your life.
   Prompt: "Help me craft a strategy for long-term personal or professional growth that aligns with my highest vision. How can I leverage current trends, technology, or opportunities?"

The Visionary Path

As we head into a future where progress moves faster than we can keep up, the only real way forward is to become visionaries in our own lives. To burn the boats. Think bigger. Think differently. And take bold risks that push the limits of what we believe is possible.

In a world where jobs, titles, industries, and entire systems will keep changing, if you're willing to step into your visionary power, you won't lose yourself—you'll discover more of who you really are.

You may not always give the world what it wants. But you'll give it what it truly needs—someone who's come fully alive.

CHAPTER 5

Deepfakes Will Deceive You: Live by Insight Not Eyesight

> There are things you know about, and things you don't,
> the known and the unknown, and in between are the doors.
>
> **Ray Manzarek**

Janet stared at the screen in disbelief. The headline read, "CEO Janet Marks Caught in Explosive Rant Against Activists!" Below it, a video played, showing a perfect replica of her, angrily attacking her political party and calling its supporters a cancer destroying the country. Many of these people were her company's biggest supporters. Some were clients. Others were friends. They were already cutting ties. Politicians were speaking out. Even some of her most loyal employees were planning to quit.

A flawless deepfake was tearing her reputation apart.

In the chaos of her unraveling world, she remembered something from a recent leadership seminar—a lesson from aviation. When pilots fly through storms and can't see, they're taught to rely on instruments instead of their eyes: “Fly by instruments, not by sight.” In her training, this was a metaphor. It meant using your inner tools—presence, intuition, clear thinking—when life gets stormy. Over the past few years, Janet had worked hard to develop that awareness. Now was the moment to use it.

She closed her eyes, centered herself, and let go of the noise. Slowly, she felt a deeper kind of knowing. No words or images, just a sense of the bigger picture. A different kind of seeing. She wasn’t flying blind anymore. She was flying by insight.

Instead of trusting AI detection tools, which had failed, she followed her intuition and started digging into the details herself. She analyzed the video, looking at metadata, reposts, and the timeline of shares across platforms. At first, everything looked real. But then she noticed a small, barely visible inconsisency in an image. Then another in some copy. Most people would’ve missed it, but not her. That one glitch cracked the illusion.

It led her to a trail of synthetic accounts—bots designed to spread the video and make it look organic. The fake had gone viral on purpose, and even the best security tools hadn’t caught it. As she kept digging, she saw a pattern. A competitor had recently been hit by a similar attack. This wasn’t a random incident—it was part of a coordinated smear campaign. Her gut had been right. She brought her team together, guided them through the evidence, and they traced the source of the deepfake to another competitor.

Relief washed over her—but only for a moment. The worst had been avoided, but the damage was still there. Some people would never forget the video. Deepfakes were becoming harder to spot. And the war between truth and illusion was only getting more dangerous.

As Janet stood at her office window, staring at the city lights, she knew she had won this round. But it was a bittersweet victory. The real fight—the fight for truth—was far from over. And it was a fight humanity couldn’t afford to lose.

Seeing Is Not Believing

While that story is fictional, the possibility of it—and worse—is very real. In fact, it's already happening. The world is entering an era where deepfakes—highly realistic AI-generated videos, voices, texts, and images—are becoming common. These fake creations can look and sound exactly like real people, even creating entire events that never happened or people who never existed.

The risk is unprecedented.

From fake news to financial scams, deepfakes are getting so real that we may soon not be able to believe our own eyes or ears.

AI-generated voice and video scams are already tricking companies and individuals, sometimes costing them millions. In one case, scammers used real-time AI to impersonate executives on a Zoom call at an Asian company.[1] They convinced employees to send $25 million. In another case, a CEO got a call from what seemed like his boss at the parent company—it was an AI-generated voice. He wired nearly $250,000. The scammers had only needed a few seconds of voice recording to create the clone.[2] A Florida man almost lost $35,000 when he got a call from someone who sounded just like his son, asking for bail money after a car accident—but it was a fake voice, too.[3]

deepfakes are getting so real that we may soon not be able to believe our own eyes or ears

And this is just the beginning.

Deepfakes take advantage of how our brains are wired. We're more likely to believe things that match what we already think—called confirmation bias. When deepfakes echo our beliefs and fears, they often only have to look and sound *real enough* for us to get hooked. As Dr. Tali Sharot and others have found, we trust what *feels* true, even when it isn't.[4] Deepfakes work because they look and sound real enough to fool us—especially when they echo our beliefs or fears.

Social media algorithms are already built to feed this kind of content. They're designed to grab attention by triggering emotion, often making us more reactive and divided. Even more dangerous is what happens when people stop trusting any media at all. If only a few groups have access to the tools to make or detect deepfakes, the power gap widens. Truth becomes a weapon—used by the few, while the rest of us are left unsure of what's real. That kind of confusion can destroy public trust, break down civil conversation, and threaten democracy itself.

If truth and fiction are impossible to tell apart, how can we make good decisions? How can we protect our identities, reputations, or rights? How can we stay sane in a world where anyone's face or voice can be copied—or worse, used against them?

if truth and fiction are impossible to tell apart, how can we make good decisions

Even more troubling, when people stop believing in anything, they often shut down. They stop caring, stop speaking up, and pull away from society. If we reach that point—where people feel powerless to know what's true—we risk more than just confusion.

We risk collapse.

Our Inner Instrument Panel

In this age of digital deception, we need to rely less on what we see or hear and more on what we sense through the power of insight. Like pilots flying through darkness using their instrument panels, we need to develop trust in our own "inner instruments." That means learning to follow our gut instinct, intuition, pattern recognition, and a kind of thinking called *first principles*—tools that help us find the truth when the world feels full of noise and confusion.

First principles thinking, a method first introduced by Aristotle, means breaking a problem down to its most basic truths and reasoning from the ground up.[5] It helps cut through false ideas, misinformation, and mental shortcuts to get to what's actually real. In a world where deepfakes can fool our senses, asking "What do I know to be true, and why?" becomes a critical way to navigate through the storm.

To think this way, we need to stay curious, humble, and open to different views. Think of the parable of the blind men and the elephant. Each man touched a different part—like the trunk or the leg—and came up with a completely different idea of what the animal was. Each one believed he was right. But they were all wrong because they were only seeing part of the truth. And even that was distorted without seeing the larger picture.

The same goes for us. We mostly live in blind spots—at best only seeing pieces of what's real. To understand more, we need to admit that our view is limited, and that truth often comes through *many* perspectives, not just one.

That includes the voices inside of us. We don't have one clear inner voice—we have many. Some speak with confidence, others whisper with doubt, fear, passion, anger, or hope. Depending on how we were raised and what's going on around us, we often ignore the ones that don't match our usual beliefs. But they're all messengers. Even discomfort in our bodies—a knot in the stomach, tightness in the chest, or tension in the jaw—is feedback. These signals may not feel pleasant, but they each hold a part of the truth.

we mostly live in blind spots—at best only seeing pieces of what's real

Like the blind men, every voice, every emotion, every sensation is touching a part of something bigger. When we listen to them all—not just the ones we like or understand—we start to see a fuller picture than our minds alone can show us.

As we explored earlier, we also have a special ability called *metacognition*, the power to think about our thinking. This allows us to pause, notice what we're feeling or assuming, and ask, "Is this really true?" Even in hard or chaotic moments, we can train ourselves to zoom out, shift our focus, and look again. We can turn the problem around in our minds and view it from another side—sometimes noticing something we never saw before.

In addition to asking "What do I know to be true, and why?" we can also ask ourselves these questions:

- "What might I not be seeing?"
- "What am I feeling that I've been avoiding?"
- "If I was looking at this for the first time, what would I notice?"
- "What would someone else see here that I'm missing?"

You can also get creative: What would a great leader, thinker, or even someone you admire say about this situation? What would they ask? What would they do?

These kinds of questions stretch your mind. They help you see more, sense more, and think more clearly. As the saying goes (paraphrasing Oliver Wendell Holmes Sr.), "Man's mind, once stretched by a new idea, never regains its original dimensions."

Every time you practice this kind of thinking, your mind gets stronger. You begin to open doors in your brain and heart that most people never even realize are there.

Becoming a Truth-Seeker and Wisdom-Keeper

Inside each of us is a deep, natural wisdom—it lives in our DNA, our instincts, our emotions, and our awareness. I call this our original AI—ancestral intelligence or ancient intelligence. To live in a world flooded with information, misinformation, and manipulation, we need to go beyond just thinking with our heads—and access this more essential way of understanding. A knowing that often comes before logic or reason takes over.

This kind of insight starts by falling in love with the question, not rushing to the answer. Albert Einstein once said, "The important thing is not to stop questioning."[6] To *live in the question* means being willing to sit with uncertainty—to stay curious in the unknown. It means accepting that much of life exists in our blind spots. For many people, this is uncomfortable. We've evolved to see and predict our environment. But as the parable of the blind men shows, we only notice a tiny slice of what's actually there.

inside each of us is a deep, natural wisdom—it lives in our DNA, our instincts, our emotions, and our awareness

As the old saying goes, "Sunlight is the best disinfectant." But darkness is where many of our wounds and worldviews begin—and where we must go to find their root. To do that, we must learn to see in the dark. That means reading between the lines, hearing the subtext, noticing what's not being said, and picking up on cues that aren't obvious.

This is called discernment—the ability to detect the truth when the surface looks convincing. It's the deeper seeing Jesus pointed to when he said, "Though seeing, they do not see; though hearing, they do not hear or understand."[7] Buddha also touched on this when he warned that people mistake what's important for what really matters.[8] And Lao Tzu taught that true understanding doesn't always require outward seeking or seeing. In fact, he said that the farther you go in that direction, the less you know.[9]

Modern research backs this up. Psychologist Daniel Kahneman showed that our brains are wired to pick up patterns—even ones we don't notice consciously.[10] With practice, we can tune in to this intuitive wisdom and begin to trust it, even when outside information is confusing or unclear.

Of course, this isn't easy. Trusting your inner vision can feel like flying blind. And for many of us, navigating through the dark triggers fear. But it doesn't have to. There are stories from Indigenous communities in Africa and the Amazon that talk of people who can find their way in total darkness, using what they call an *inner vision*. Some believe this comes from activating the pineal gland—sometimes called the "third eye"—which responds to light like an actual eye and is linked to deeper, even spiritual, awareness.[11]

trusting your inner vision can feel like flying blind

This shows that our minds and bodies can adapt in powerful ways—if we let them.[12] But in modern life, we rarely spend time in the dark. Cities glow with artificial lights. Screens fill our eyes with endless information. We don't need to sit in uncertainty anymore—so we've lost some of our ability to handle it.[13] The more we light up our world, the less we actually *see*.

It's like the old Sufi parable of Mulla Nasrudin, who is seen searching on the ground for his lost key. A man comes along and joins him in the search, but after a long, fruitless hunt, the man asks, "Where exactly did you drop it?" Nasrudin replies, "In my house." Baffled, the man asks, "Then why are you looking here?" Nasrudin responds matter-of-factly, "There is more light here than inside my house."[14]

Ancient stories and modern psychology—like the work of Carl Jung—all point to the same idea: the solutions to our deepest problems are hidden in the places we avoid. The shadow, the unknown, the parts of ourselves and the world we don't want to face—that's where transformation lives.[15]

To get that vision back—to *see in the dark*—we must turn down the artificial light. We must step away from constant notifications, quick answers, and shiny distractions. We must be willing to enter the mystery and let our inner compass guide us.

That's how we learn to see what's real.

That's how we find our way back.

Becoming a Modern-Day Jedi

To truly live by insight takes a kind of Jedi training. It's more than just using your brain—it's about tapping into a deeper guidance that's always been inside you. It means learning to see beneath the surface, to tune out the noise of everyday life and connect with something greater. Call it the "Force" or what spiritual traditions describe as *universal intelligence*—it's an inner light that can lead you through darkness, chaos, and uncertainty.

This journey is similar to what students went through in ancient mystery schools. These were places of deep spiritual training that existed in Egypt, Greece, and other cultures. Students in these schools went through challenges and practices meant to wake up their inner powers and sharpen their deeper senses.[16] Like Jedi training, it wasn't just about mastering the visible world—it was about awakening a different kind of awareness.

an inner light that can lead you through darkness, chaos, and uncertainty

They believed humans weren't limited to the mind or body but were connected to a greater web of life. Many of our biggest breakthroughs in human history came from this. The Greeks, for example, discovered geometry and philosophy through insight, intuition, and reflection. These ideas laid the foundation for modern science, math, and philosophy—systems that still shape our world today.[17]

I know this might sound a little lofty or out of reach. Most of us, including me, rarely have the time to go deep into ancient training or reach total self-mastery. But the good news is we don't have to. We're already building on the energy and wisdom of those who came before. The signal from the universe—the Force—is with you. And it's stronger than ever. If you're willing to make even a little space in this loud, busy world, you can reconnect with that forgotten part of yourself.

Modern neuroscience now supports this. Research shows that simple habits like mindfulness and meditation can unlock these deeper powers.[18] Studies have found that meditation strengthens the prefrontal cortex—the part of your brain that helps you make decisions, stay calm, and think clearly. Meditation can also grow gray matter in the hippocampus, which helps with memory and learning. This means your brain becomes better at handling complex ideas and less likely to get overwhelmed or tricked by misinformation.

And thanks to *neuroplasticity*—your brain's ability to reshape and renew itself—you can rebuild these skills and get back what's been lost.[19] You can become grounded in truth. Hear the signal in the noise. See through the clouds. And defeat the Dark Side!

defeat the Dark Side

How to Use AI to Activate This Human Evolution

The key is not to let technology become your only guide. Don't hand over your instincts to AI or let it replace your eyes and ears. That dulls your natural power to sense and see.

In the final battle of the original *Star Wars*, when everything seemed lost, Luke turned off his targeting system and trusted the Force. That's what helped him see what machines couldn't—and hit an impossible target.

To become a modern-day Jedi, and detect the truth in the noise, we must do the same. We can still use tech to help sharpen our vision. But in the end, we must learn to trust that deeper sense within us to cut through the fog and confusion and see what matters most.

become a modern-day Jedi

To use the prompts below, enter them into the same AI chat you've been journaling with. That way, it remembers your past answers and gives more thoughtful feedback. If you're starting fresh, just ask the AI what it needs to know to help you better.

1. **Self-Reflection and Discernment**
   What to Supply AI: Share details about a current situation where you need to make a decision. Include what you believe or feel about it—especially anything you feel very sure or strongly about.
   Prompt: "Help me identify any cognitive biases that might be affecting my current decision-making process and how I can counteract them."

2. **Deepening Insight**
   What to Supply AI: You can use the same issue as before, add more details, or share something new you want help understanding through your intuition.
   Prompt: "Guide me through an exercise that helps me tap into my intuition. How can I practice trusting my inner knowing when faced with conflicting information?"

3. **First Principles Thinking**
   What to Supply AI: You can use the earlier issue, add extra information or feelings, or share a new problem you'd like to understand in a different way.
   Prompt: "Help me break down a complex problem using first principles thinking. What are the fundamental truths about this issue?"

4. **Navigating Conflicting Information**
   What to Supply AI: Share a situation where you've received different or opposite points of view. Include as many of those viewpoints as possible.

Prompt: "Show me how to triangulate between multiple conflicting sources of information to find the most accurate or reliable truth."

5. **Activate Your Superintelligence**
   What to Supply AI: Share more about your personal life, daily habits, and anything that's been on your mind or heart. You can also ask the AI to consider everything you've shared in earlier prompts when giving its response.
   Prompt: "What are the top habits or daily practices I can develop to enhance my mental clarity, focus, and insight?"

Living by the Signal Instead of the Noise

In a world of deepfakes and digital illusions, we can't rely on eyesight alone. We must live by insight—by learning to sense the *signal* in the noise. This means going deeper. Past the surface. Past first impressions. Toward what's real.

It takes practice. The truth often whispers. It hides in small signs—shifts in tone, timing, or the feeling behind the facts. You must listen with more than your ears. You need your gut. Your heart. Your inner radar. And you need courage—to pause before reacting. To question what you're told. To sit with the discomfort of not knowing.

humility and curiosity are now superpowers

We're entering an age of intelligent deception. Where even our own thoughts can be manipulated. That's why humility and curiosity are now superpowers. We must stop fearing the dark and learn to walk through it with steady feet.

When the world turns us around and nothing feels clear, our developed inner compass will guide us. And if we are willing to walk by that inner light, we won't just find our way through—we'll become wayshowers. Helping others find their way back home.

When the world turns us around and nothing feels clear, our developed inner compass will guide us

CHAPTER 6

AI Will Expose You: Become Transparent

You are only afraid if you are not in harmony with yourself.

Hermann Hesse

In the late 2000s, British singer Robbie Williams was followed by paparazzi so much it nearly broke him.[1] But instead of hiding or fighting back, he flipped the script—he started telling photographers exactly where he'd be and when. By dropping his defenses, he took away their power to catch him off guard. The "gotcha" moments stopped. He realized real freedom wouldn't come from running or resisting. It would come from owning the truth—so no one could use it against him.

In 2017, actor and comedian Kevin Hart went through something similar. When he got caught in a cheating scandal, he didn't wait for the media to drag him through the mud. He grabbed the mic—and shared his side on social media. He admitted his mistake, apologized to his family, and vowed to do better. He didn't spin it or blame anyone.[2] At first, the public was upset. But because he was real and vulnerable, many respected him more. By speaking out first, he disarmed the critics. And by being open and honest, he was able to rebuild trust and move on without the fear of being exposed.

No More Secrets

Every part of your life—your online activity, money records, and private messages—is now at risk of being seen by others. With AI, personal data can be gathered, sorted, and shared faster than ever. Algorithms can already piece together your habits, likes, and even your most private thoughts—just from little bits of data.[3]

As technology speeds up, no area of your life will be fully private. This battle over privacy is going to be one of the biggest personal and social struggles we face. The trust that holds society together is already breaking apart. As people get more scared, the natural response is to build stronger security: bigger firewalls, better encryption, smarter AI. That's already happening. And with quantum computers on the horizon, the race to protect (and hack) your privacy will only grow faster.

as technology speeds up, no area of your life will be fully private

Of course, we need security. We need to protect our money, our ideas, our identities. But the more we rely on AI to keep us safe, the more we risk losing our freedom. Instead of living real, open lives, we could end up living small ones—afraid to be seen. In our attempt to protect ourselves, we could end up building a surveillance state where there's nowhere to hide—and a digital prison where there's no escape.

Instead of building bigger walls around us, we should ask two deeper questions. First: *What am I trying so hard to protect—and why?* Beyond bank accounts or health records, most of what we hide is tied to shame or fear of being judged. Second: *Who would I have to become to have nothing left to hide?* That's a tough one. But if we can answer it honestly, it might lead to one of the most powerful breakthroughs of our lives. It means learning to live in such truth that even if everyone knew everything about us, we could still hold our heads high. That's the real hero's journey. The one that sets us free. Not being perfect. But facing our fears and being honest with ourselves.

To be fair, some people say we shouldn't have to live this way. We deserve privacy. The more open we are, the more it gives bad actors and governments a chance to control or punish us. I agree—this is a serious issue. But we may not have the luxury of choosing anymore. So, we have to learn how to live with freedom and power no matter what.

Some people also worry that being real could make others reject them. And yes, that can happen. People are judgmental. And in a world that loves to take others down, it's scary to be fully seen. But much of the pain we feel isn't just about others—it's about how we judge ourselves. Hiding from that takes a toll. Often, more than being real ever would.

And let's be clear—being transparent doesn't mean telling everyone everything. It doesn't mean oversharing or shouting your deepest secrets to the world. Discernment still matters. Just because you feel something doesn't mean you have to say it. Just because you did something in private doesn't mean you owe the world an explanation. Being transparent means knowing and accepting yourself so fully that even if your private diary leaked, you wouldn't panic—you'd respond from wisdom, not fear. From self-compassion, not shame.

Becoming Defenseless Is Our Greatest Defense

From ancient myths to modern action movies, we're taught that the warrior is the ideal hero. They gain power and safety by becoming stronger, tougher, and harder to hurt. The problem is, this kind of power says you must avoid being vulnerable, never admit you're wrong, and always look like you have it all together. It creates the image of someone who's impossible to break—but that's not real strength. In fact, this kind of thinking leads people and even whole societies into cycles of emotional shutdown, conflict, and collapse.

As AI grows more powerful, we need a new kind of strength. Pushing back with force doesn't stop algorithms from manipulating us. In fact, the harder we fight, the more we can get pulled into arguments that weaken us—and break down the trust that holds us together. But when someone chooses not to fight—when they get curious, open up, and show their real selves—the cycle can stop. Some people (and yes, even bots) may still try to attack, but others will lower their defenses.

pushing back with force doesn't stop algorithms from manipulating us

I've seen this myself. When I've been attacked online and listened openly—instead of fighting back—some of the harshest critics backed down. A few were even moved by my honest replies. And sometimes, they even started defending me or reflecting on their own behavior. In those moments, something human was restored.

With AI everywhere, causing more people to fight for their lives—and likes—our power won't come from "owning them" or "dunking on them." It'll come from being real—with ourselves and others. When we own our flaws and fears and stop acting like we've got it all figured out, we disarm critics and make deeper connections. We even turn some enemies into allies. In a world full of people trying to trap others in "gotcha" moments, our best defense might be letting go of the need to defend at all.

When we allow ourselves to be vulnerable—admitting we're imperfect and still learning—we unlock a strength most people never tap into. Researcher and author Brené Brown says vulnerability isn't weakness. It's the starting point of real connection and emotional resilience.[4] Hiding who we are creates a gap between how we feel inside and how we show up on the outside. And that gap can make us feel anxious, alone, or even depressed. But when we're open about our struggles, it lifts the heavy weight of shame. Sharing our truth can make us feel more whole—and allows others to meet us with more trust and openness. This is true in friendships, in family, and even at work.

Leaders like Gandhi, Martin Luther King Jr., and Nelson Mandela knew this. They didn't win by force. Their strength came from standing for what they believed in and being honest—even when it made them vulnerable. That's why people followed them. Not because they were the toughest, but because they were the most human. When leaders show up like this, they create trust, spark creativity, and help people work together in more inspired ways.

hiding who we are creates a gap between how we feel inside and how we show up on the outside

In a world where people are losing trust in almost everything—governments, media, even each other—this kind of leadership matters more than ever. If we want to fix what's broken, we can't do it by force or defense. We have to start by being honest and authentic. That's how we rebuild things with truth and integrity, instead of tearing them apart with blame and fear.

When We Have Nothing to Hide, We Can Finally Be Seen

Of course, the deeper kind of strength shown by Gandhi, King, and Mandela isn't the norm. And it doesn't mean we never need to protect ourselves. Sometimes we do, even forcefully, especially when others mean harm and refuse to respect laws or human decency. But it's also possible to go too far. We can build such thick armor that we shut out the very things that could help us grow.

Today, with media and AI always ready to expose flaws and secrets, many people—famous or not—live in constant defense. They're afraid of being "found out." The fear of public shame or being "canceled" leads people to hide their real selves. That creates a world of mistrust. The strange part is that what we fear most is also what we need most—to be seen. But in our constant drive to look perfect and never let 'em see us sweat, we stay stuck in a downward spiral that robs us of the thing we most desire.

If we want real connection and to feel truly seen, we must be brave enough to lower our walls and stop hiding. Psychologist Carl Rogers, who created client-centered therapy, called this "unconditional positive regard."[5] It's the power of feeling fully accepted, even with flaws. When someone embraces the real you, it builds deep trust. This kind of trust helps us grow and feel safe to be even more ourselves.

Another psychologist, John Bowlby, found something similar with his attachment theory.[6] He showed that kids feel secure when their caregivers are consistent, loving, and present. That safety in childhood builds the foundation for healthy adult relationships. If someone grows up with mixed signals or judgment, they often develop fear around being real—and learn to protect themselves by hiding.

If you had this kind of upbringing, it might feel like it's too late. Like you're just broken. And looking out at the world, you might decide that it's so full of these broken, scared, and defensive people that there's no way to show who you really are. But the truth is, you don't need others to be different to get what you need. You just need to have the courage to see and accept yourself.

Real transparency starts when we face the parts of us we've been ignoring, hiding, or criticizing. Most of the time, we fear others' judgment because we're already judging ourselves. This is called projection—when we push away the things we don't like about ourselves and blame them on others instead. This reinforces the belief that others need to change

real transparency starts when we face the parts of us we've been ignoring, hiding, or criticizing

before we can be safe enough to be seen. And it creates more distance between them and ourselves.

The secret is to embrace these hidden, rejected aspects inside you. What Carl Jung called our "shadows."[7] These are unconscious beliefs about parts of ourselves that have been acting out, trying to get our attention. And when we bring them into the light, we take away their power to run the show. We also stop putting them on others and creating more conflict. The fact is, a lot of the division we see in the world today comes from people projecting their inner fears and wounds onto others. But we can break that cycle. We just need to meet those parts of ourselves with honesty and compassion. When we can hold them and hear them . . . we can finally heal them.

Psychologist Kristin Neff, who studies self-compassion, says we need to treat ourselves like we'd treat a close friend—especially when we mess up or feel insecure.[8] The golden rule says, "Love your neighbor as yourself." But maybe we need a diamond rule too: "Love yourself the way you wish others would love you."

Keeping secrets can damage both our minds and bodies. Dr. Michael Slepian, a psychologist at Columbia, found that hiding secrets creates stress, anxiety, and loneliness—even if no one else knows them.[9] Just thinking about our secrets can make us feel ashamed and disconnected from who we really are. This fear of being "seen" may have helped us survive in the past—back when being kicked out of the tribe meant real danger. But now it keeps us from becoming stronger, wiser, and more whole in a world that's changing fast.

That's why transparency—with ourselves first, and then with others—is so important.

Dr. James Pennebaker studied this and found that writing about our hidden thoughts and feelings improves both mental and physical health.[10] Sharing our truth, even just with ourselves, lowers stress, strengthens our immune system, and helps us feel more real. It starts a healing process.

That old saying "the truth will set you free" has real power. When we tell the truth, we unlock the cage we've built inside.

But this kind of freedom means we need to let go of the armor we've used to protect ourselves. We have to tear down the wall between our private and public selves and own our whole story. Because it's that full, real version of you—the one you don't think is worthy or lovable—that holds the latent talents, gifts, and abilities that will make you truly irreplaceable. What's more, when you let your freak flag fly, even a little, you'll give everyone around you permission to do the same.

we have to tear down the wall between our private and public selves and own our whole story

When You're Transparent, There's Nothing to Attack

As we've talked about, when we choose transparency, we have fewer secrets to hide—and there's less for critics or AI systems to use against us. When we own our truth and admit our flaws, we take away the power of those who try to control us through fear. When we choose to be in a vulnerable state is when we become *invulnerable*. That's the paradox. And when we're honest about our struggles and imperfections and take full responsibility for our lives, we don't just free ourselves—we free others to do the same. That's how transparency becomes contagious. The more it spreads, the more it weakens manipulative systems—whether from the media, corporations, or algorithms—and the more it builds real connection and trust.

We saw this play out online with the rise of what some called the "intellectual dark web," where a group of podcasters and thought leaders started speaking openly about cultural and political topics that had been considered off-limits. Their honest—if not always accurate—perspectives broke through the media's tight control over information. People started considering new points of view, having the courage to share their own, and challenging the official narratives. It opened a floodgate.

With so much more open expression, however, came more harmful ideas too. Some facts got blurred. Some things were just false. More confusion was created. And trust in institutions eroded. And that's a real problem we don't want to take lightly. Without a trusted way to separate fact from fiction, we don't get more truth—we get more chaos. Tearing down all the structures of society doesn't create freedom—it creates a power vacuum. That leads to people turning to strong, controlling leaders to bring order back. And that's how dictatorships can rise.

tearing down all the structures of society doesn't create freedom—it creates a power vacuum

Still, even with these risks, something important was set in motion. This wave of radical honesty opened doors that had long been locked. It pushed past gatekeepers who once controlled what was allowed to be said, shown, or known. Their grip is slipping. Legacy media no longer fully control the story. That gives individuals more power to come out from hiding—but it also means more responsibility.

Because the truth is, real freedom isn't just about saying whatever you want. To as large a crowd as you can. It's about being free to live authentically, yes. And make your unique contribution. But it also requires the willingness to accept opposing ideas. Not to censor you but to refine you. And that's not easy. Or glamorous. It's not Instagram famous. It's real life. It has real costs. But it might just be worth it.

As more people share who they are, and are met with curiosity and constructive feedback, we can discover more about ourselves and each other than any one person could. If we can be brave enough to be ourselves and accept others who do the same, we can create a society where it's safe to be different. Not just safe but celebrated. All the algorithms and media that use our weakness as weapons would be powerless. Imagine what would be possible then?

It will be messy and uncomfortable. Not everyone will play along. At least at first. But as more people choose this level of transparency—flawed and imperfect as it may be—trust can begin to grow again. Instead of seeing each other as enemies or stereotypes, we might start seeing each other as real, whole human beings. And in that fearless (if fragile) space between honesty and acceptance, something new could take root—not just the safety to be ourselves, but the kind of seeing and being seen that makes true belonging possible.

The Path to Transparency

Becoming transparent means aligning your private self with your public self—so who you are behind the scenes matches who you are in the world. That way, if anything is revealed, there's no shock, shame, or fear.

This doesn't mean you have to share every personal detail. It just means living in a way where there's nothing major to hide. When what you say, believe, and do are all in sync, the fear of being exposed fades—because you're no longer a house divided.

Here's a simple, practical plan to bring more transparency into your life. It starts with being honest with yourself, and then expands into how you show up in your relationships, your work, and your online presence.

Step 1: Personal Honesty

Look at the parts of you that you usually hide—things you might feel ashamed of or afraid others will judge. These hidden thoughts or past actions can cause stress and anxiety. But when you face them with compassion, they lose power over you. The goal is to live in harmony with yourself—where what you think, feel, and do all line up. This brings more peace inside and less fear of being exposed.

Step 2: Integrity in Relationships

Being transparent in your relationships means being real, even when it's hard. Talk honestly with your friends, family, or your partner. Share your struggles. Admit your mistakes. This kind of honesty builds stronger trust, deeper connection, and frees you from having to pretend or hide.

being transparent in your relationships means being real, even when it's hard

Step 3: Professional Integrity

At work, transparency means living your values and being accountable. Own your mistakes. Speak openly and honestly—making sure all needs, concerns, or expectations are clear. No brushing under the rug. No dancing around the issue. It may take more effort, but it'll build real trust and respect with others and yourself. And ensure your goals and career match who you really are.

Step 4: Digital Transparency

Online, be the same person you are offline. Don't try to create a perfect image or hide behind filters. Make sure your posts and profiles reflect your real values and identity. Living this way builds confidence and helps you avoid the stress of managing a fake persona.

don't try to create a perfect image or hide behind filters

Step 5: Embrace Transparency Daily

Living transparently isn't a one-time thing—it's a daily practice. Keep checking in with yourself. Notice when you're hiding something or being inauthentic, and gently bring yourself back into alignment. You don't have to be perfect—just real.

You may feel fear or discomfort along the way, and others might not always understand your openness. But if you keep showing up with honesty and compassion, your life will feel lighter, freer, and more connected. You'll earn deeper trust, build stronger relationships, and feel more whole.

in a world where privacy is harder to protect, the freedom that comes from having nothing to hide might just be the greatest freedom of all

When you live transparently, no one can use your truth against you—because you've already owned it. In a world where privacy is harder to protect, the freedom that comes from having nothing to hide might just be the greatest freedom of all.

How to Use AI to Activate This Human Evolution

Becoming transparent takes more than good intentions. It requires steady effort, honest self-reflection, and staying accountable. AI can help support this journey—offering tools to track your progress, stay aligned with your values, and live with more integrity every day.

1. **Self-Reflection and Personal Honesty**
   What to Supply AI: Share situations where you've felt shame, guilt, or fear. Describe times when you hid your real thoughts or actions. Focus on areas of your life that feel tense, secretive, or unresolved—and reflect on why.
   Prompt: "What parts of my life am I hiding from myself or others? What beliefs or fears are keeping me from being fully transparent?"

2. **Integrity in Relationships**
   What to Supply AI: Provide examples of strained conversations, hidden emotions, or things you've avoided saying. Share your

hopes for improving connections with others and what's been hard for you to talk about.
Prompt: "How can I be more honest in my relationships? What tough conversation am I avoiding—and how can I begin it?"

3. **Daily Vulnerability Challenge**
   What to Supply AI: Share something you've struggled with emotionally, especially recently. Then name one person you'd like to be more open with—and why.
   Prompt: "What truth can I share with someone today? How can opening up deepen our connection?"

4. **Professional Transparency and Accountability**
   What to Supply AI: Describe moments at work when you acted out of alignment with your values. Share specific decisions or situations that left you feeling uneasy or regretful.
   Prompt: "Did my actions at work reflect my real values today? How can I bring more honesty and integrity into my professional life?"

5. **Digital Footprint Alignment**
   What to Supply AI: List or summarize your online posts and content honestly—without trying to edit or spin them. Then reflect on whether they reflect your true self.
   Prompt: "Does my online persona match who I really am? Where might I be showing a version of myself that isn't fully aligned?"

6. **Accountability and Progress Tracking**
   What to Supply AI: Reflect on where you've practiced transparency this week—and where you've held back. Be specific about your wins and your sticking points.

Prompt: "Where did I shrink back from full transparency—and how can I stretch farther next time?"

Becoming an Undivided Person in a Divided World

When we try to serve both our true self and the persona we've crafted for survival, we become a house divided. And a divided house cannot stand. It lacks integrity—structurally, psychologically, emotionally, and spiritually.

While the world seems to spin off its axis, with people polarized and hypnotized by algorithms, our first responsibility is to get our own house in order. By cleaning up our own dirty laundry, we reclaim personal power, confidence, and character—giving us the clarity and courage to walk our true path.

We become sovereigns of our own lives, rooted in self-love, seated firmly on the throne of our hearts, able to govern ourselves with integrity and serve others generously.

In a world increasingly defined by technology and the erosion of privacy, radical transparency won't just be a defensive stance or a tool of offense—it will become one of the boldest steps in our human evolution.

we become catalysts for a world where trust, connection, and honesty have room to flourish once again

Freed from the burden of secrecy and the energy it drains, we will develop immunity to the judgment and control of external forces.

In doing so, we become catalysts for a world where trust, connection, and honesty have room to flourish once again.

CHAPTER 7

AI Will Widen the Wealth Gap: Build an Abundance Mindset

We make a living by what we get,
but we make a life by what we give
Anonymous

In the late 1990s, when most startups were still run by tech and finance bros and few women were getting funding, a young woman named Sara Blakely was stuck selling fax machines door to door. She felt like she was meant for more. But there was no clear roadmap. She didn't have a business degree or investors. There were no insider contacts or fancy mentors whispering startup secrets over matcha.

All she had was $5,000 in savings. A dream. And the will to never give up.

Then one day, after cutting the feet off a pair of pantyhose, she realized she'd discovered something a lot of women wanted—comfortable, body-slimming undergarments. She didn't know it then, but her idea would become a lasting symbol of confidence, possibility, and self-made success: Spanx.

At first, people laughed or dismissed her, but she didn't back down. She called hosiery mills and was rejected for months until one owner—pushed by his daughters—agreed to give her a shot. She wrote her own patent. Designed her own packaging. And shipped orders out of her tiny Atlanta apartment.[1]

Her friends and family became her first fans and test group, drawn to the product not just because it worked but because it gave them a feeling of power, freedom, and being more at home in their skin. Still, Sara was turned down by every major store.

She knew she had something, though. So, she pitched buyers face to face, gave product demos in bathroom stalls, and faked a PR buzz by having friends walk into shops and ask for Spanx by name.

The energy grew and word spread until one day, Oprah came calling. She featured the product on her show—and just like that, everything changed. Sara kept full ownership of the company. She never took outside funding. And she grew Spanx into a billion-dollar brand.

But this wasn't just a business win. It was a story about what happens when one person believes there's more than enough—enough opportunity, enough space, enough possibility—for them to create something valuable.

That's the abundance mindset.

Sara Blakely exemplified the truth that you don't need permission, perfection, or a trust fund to build something big. She didn't wait for the stars to align. She believed in herself and her vision. And moved anyway. Where others saw lack, she saw potential. Where others stayed small to fit in, she stretched the world around her—and built something that helped other people feel like they fit too.

you don't need permission, perfection, or a trust fund to build something big

She didn't just reshape undergarments. She reshaped success itself—for millions of women.

Closing the Wealth Gap Within

While many AI experts say that the future will bring more abundance for everyone, they often leave something out. At first—and maybe for a long time—the gap between the rich and poor will grow. That is what's happened in every industrial revolution. The rich get richer, the poor get poorer, and the wealthy say it's all for the greater good.[2] But regular people rarely, if ever, see those benefits during their working years.

Job loss, reskilling, and lifestyle changes are often too much for many people to handle. Those who aren't prepared ahead of time are more likely to fall behind. And it's not just about losing jobs. This growing gap between the haves and have-nots can lead to deeper issues—like losing a sense of purpose or becoming more dependent on technology and government. That creates even more disconnection and powerlessness.

But inside this crisis is a hidden opportunity—a chance for deep personal and collective change. An evolution of what wealth and power really are. Hint: it's not what we've been taught. It's not money or status. Not the size of your house or the number of people who listen when you speak. It's not about control over the world out there at all. It's about connection to the world inside. We've all seen so many examples of this, it's a cliché. People with everything, still feeling like nothing. Celebrities falling apart under the weight of all their gold. Mansions full of broken marriages, broken families, and broken hearts.

people with everything, still feeling like nothing

That doesn't mean it's wrong to want nice things—or to have enough of whatever supports your life. But when we believe that success lives out there, we start building our life on sand. We chase what we think we need to be okay. Trade parts of our soul to feel secure or stay in control. And somewhere along the way, we lose ourselves.

Remember the movie *Citizen Kane*? He had everything—but on his deathbed, all he wanted was the sled from his childhood. *Rosebud*. Why? Because it reminded him of a time when he felt free. Unburdened. And truly alive. At the end of the day, or the end of a life, that's all any of us really want. Not deeper pockets—but a deeper peace the world can't give us. Not all the things we think will finally fill us up—but a true fulfillment that only we can give ourselves.

That's the only thing that will ever make us feel truly rich.

That's the heart of abundance.

And when a crisis threatens what we have or strips away the things we thought we needed, it's not the end. It's the beginning. A chance to come home to yourself again. And find that you have more than you ever imagined.

But we don't have to wait for a breakdown—we can come back to ourselves now. We can reconnect to the source within us. Before we separated. Before we became afraid. Before we had to survive. We can live from the inside out. From a deep well that never dries up. From the life force that created everything—and can become anything we need. More love. More inspiration. More freedom. And, yes, even more money, opportunity, people, and beautiful things.

The source of life is inexhaustible.

Nature reflects this. Trees don't grow "just enough" leaves to survive. The beaches don't have "just enough" sand. And the sky isn't sprinkled with "just enough" stars. There's always more—more than we can count, or even take in. And when a tree sheds its leaves or a field lies fallow, we don't panic. We know it will bloom again.

the source of life is inexhaustible

This truth has been shared across spiritual traditions. Jesus said that birds don't store food in barns, yet they're fed. And lilies, without trying, are clothed more beautifully than kings.[3] He was showing us that trusting life's natural abundance frees us from fear. The Buddha taught something similar:

that real contentment comes not from gaining more, but from letting go.[4] And Lao Tzu said the Tao nourishes all things without effort.[5]

These teachings all point to the same truth: when we reconnect to the source of life within, we access a kind of wealth the world didn't give us. And can never take away. And from there, we can create more than enough—limited only by our belief in what's possible.

Awakened Wealth

The poet Robert Browning wrote of "opening out a way whence the imprisoned splendor may escape,"[6] about how the creative force of life is not something we must acquire from the world, but something already within us, seeking expression. And the Gospel of Thomas echoes that truth: "If you bring forth what is within you, what you bring forth will save you. If you do not bring it forth, what you do not bring forth will destroy you."[7] In my book *Emergence*, I share a similar idea: Whatever we're waiting for, we're also waiting with—and holding back.[8] And whatever is missing is something we're not giving.

Put simply, all lack in our life is a sign of unexpressed potential.

In *The Abundance Project*, I describe something called Awakened Wealth. It's the idea that real wealth isn't about how much money you have or what you achieve on the outside. It comes from your connection to something deeper—the limitless life force within you.[9] When we realize this, we move from a scarcity mindset, rooted in fear and competition, to an abundance mindset, where possibility is unlimited.

True wealth doesn't come from constant effort or hustle. It comes from being aligned within ourselves and understanding the principles for unlocking our hidden capacities.

Think of it like an apple tree. It doesn't produce fruit by trying harder—it bears fruit every season because it's in harmony with nature. The same goes for us. When we're in sync with life, abundance flows naturally. Prosperity becomes the result of living from this deeper source. Not something we chase, but something we express.

Most people are taught that success comes from getting more, doing more, and achieving more. And yes, action is important. But if it all comes from the outside in, we end up burned out, stressed, and always feeling behind. Awakened Wealth flips that idea. It's not about getting something from out there, it's about letting what's inside you come out.

That's the real measure of abundance—not how much flows to you, but how much flows *from* you.

I call this shift the Great Reversal. Instead of thinking we're separate beings trying to get things from the world, we start to understand we're already connected to everything we need. Our real job is to let it out—through our thoughts, our actions, and our creativity.

that's the real measure of abundance—not how much flows to you, but how much flows *from* you

Another key idea is that wealth is invisible. It's the life force, intelligence, and creative energy that animates everything. Money and stuff are just symbols of it. They're not the source—they're the result. Just like an apple isn't the source of a tree's abundance, it's the expression of the energy inside it.

So, even when life is hard or money feels tight, that inner source is still there.

It can't be taken from you or worn out. It's infinite, waiting to be tapped.

Long ago, people understood this. In the days of bartering, the value of something wasn't just in the object—it was in the life force behind it. The baker knew her bread wasn't just flour and water—it was time, energy, and care. When she traded it for candles, it wasn't just a loaf for a light—it was an exchange of energy. But as society began creating a medium of exchange, using shells, gold, salt (where the word salary comes from), and later paper money[10]—we started losing that direct connection.

Eventually, currency became more abstract and was controlled by banks and governments.[11] Money became the store of value instead of people—and they forgot that they were the source, not the system. This led to a widespread belief that there wasn't enough to go around. Scarcity took hold. People started fearing the future, hoarding resources, and competing against each other. And stress and struggle over this external symbol—money—became normal.

But Awakened Wealth gives us a way out. When we know we're connected to something boundless inside, we stop living in fear and lack. We stop needing to compete or compare. We trust that our success doesn't take away from anyone else—and in fact, when more people share their gifts, the world gets richer for everyone.

You can think of this inner wealth as a kind of "trust account" inside you. It holds your wisdom, creativity, energy, and power. No matter how much you draw from it, there's always more. And the more you trust it, the stronger it grows. When you live from that place—especially in a world shaped by AI and constant change—your prosperity doesn't shrink. It expands. Because you're no longer waiting for permission or perfect timing.

when more people share their gifts, the world gets richer for everyone

You're creating from a source that never runs out.

The Law of Circulation

One of the keys to unlocking more abundance is the Law of Circulation, which says, "Things must flow to stay alive" and "The more you flow, the more you grow." Just like water gets stale when it stops moving, our wealth—whether it's money, ideas, love, or energy—needs to keep flowing or it dries up. And the more we flow any of those qualities, the more they multiply. Even the word *affluent* comes from a Latin root meaning "to flow abundantly." And currency comes from a word meaning "to flow."[12]

This idea shows up in economics too. There's something called *the velocity of money*, which is the pace money moves through the economy.[13] The faster it flows—through spending, investing, and giving—the more it helps everyone and everything grow. Another idea called *the multiplier effect* shows that one dollar, when it moves from person to person or business to business, keeps creating more value along the way.[14] The Law of Circulation works the same way: the more we let our time, talents, or treasure move out into the world, the more abundance flows back to us—and keeps on flowing.

As I mentioned in chapter 1, during the Great Depression, the biggest problem wasn't a lack of resources. There was plenty of food and goods—but people were so afraid they stopped moving them. Farms threw food away, and train cars full of produce were dumped or burned.[15] The economy didn't collapse from lack—it collapsed from a lack of flow.

When life stops moving—whether it's money, creativity, air, water, blood, or anything else—things break down. But when we give freely, from whatever we have inside or out, we open new channels. Energy starts circulating again. And where there's more circulation, there's more life and more growth.

the more we let our time, talents, or treasure move out into the world, the more abundance flows back to us—and keeps on flowing

This is the core of the abundance mindset.

It creates a new kind of wealth that's not based on winning or hoarding, but on sharing what's inside us. It's not a zero-sum game, where someone's gain is someone else's loss. It's an infinite-sum game, where everyone grows by giving. In a world where people may feel powerless under big tech and fast-moving AI, this mindset gives us back our power. Because we're not just waiting for someone to give us something—we become the source of what we need.

This doesn't just change how we feel. It changes how we relate to each other. Instead of seeing people as competition—or as things to use—we see them as partners in the flow. We stop making deals just to get something—and start building relationships that make more for everyone. That's the real circulation of abundance: not just the flow of money changing hands, but the flow of hearts, minds, and souls changing lives.

The Seven Gifts That Give You Everything

Once you understand that everything you need is already within you—and that the more you let it flow, the more you'll have—the next step is learning exactly how to start that flow. When you practice these steps, you open every channel of circulation in your life.

1. **Giving Out:** This is about giving your time, talent, and treasure to others through service, tithing, charitable donations, or other acts that share your gifts. The act of adding value to others generates an immediate flow of wealth back into your life.

2. **Giving Away:** We often hold on to material things that no longer serve us. The stack of magazines we'll never read, the boxes of stuff we'll never use. All of this is stuck energy. When you release this clutter, giving it to those who might need it or even just throwing it away, you allow new energy to flood into your life.

3. **Giving Up:** We also hold on to mental clutter, such as recurring thoughts of blame, shame, and complaint. Although everyone experiences these types of thoughts from time to time, if we don't

let them go, they quickly become stuck energy patterns that keep us in a matrix of lack. Acknowledge these thoughts, give them up to the universe, and watch the new, inspiring ideas that flow in and the new opportunities that emerge.

4. **Giving In:** This is about aligning with your true purpose and passion. When you yield to your authentic desires and inner calling, instead of holding on to what's safe and familiar, the universe will rush in and support you in ways you never imagined.

5. **Giving Thanks:** When you cultivate a practice of giving thanks, appreciating what you have, no matter how small, and even things you perceive as "bad," you activate a mindset of having and amplify the flow of abundance. What you appreciate appreciates.

6. **Giving to Yourself:** This gift is about self-care and honoring your own needs and desires. Often, we give so much to others that we neglect ourselves. By giving yourself the love, time, and resources you need, you fill your cup and have even more to give.

7. **Forgiving (For-Giving):** Holding on to grudges or resentments puts you in debt to yourself and others, blocking the flow of good into your life. Behind every chronic debt, there is a story of unforgiveness. When you forgive others and yourself, you clear the channel for more love, peace, and prosperity to enter.

The more you give, in all these forms, the more life gives back to you. When you master these gifts, you tap into a boundless source of abundance that can transform every area of your life.

Design an Abundant Environment

We're deeply shaped by the people around us. Motivational speaker Jim Rohn once said, "You become the average of the five people you spend the most time with."[16] That means the beliefs, attitudes, and habits of the people in your life will rub off on you—whether you realize it or not. If you spend time with people who always focus on what's missing or what could go wrong, you'll start thinking that way too. But if you're around people who believe in growth, who stay positive and see possibility, that way of thinking will start to become your own.

But it's not just people who shape us. Our environment—our homes, workspaces, social feeds, books, and other media we consume—also affects how we feel and think. A messy, loud, or stressful space can make it hard to feel inspired or focused. But a space that reflects your values—organized, peaceful, uplifting—helps you feel aligned and energized. That's why it matters who and what we surround ourselves with. Every voice, every space, every piece of content plays a role in shaping our inner world—and that inner world becomes the life we live.

If you're constantly watching fear-based news or scrolling social media that fuels anger or comparison, it can quietly train your brain to believe the world is dangerous or unfair. But if you fill your time with books, podcasts, or videos about growth, purpose, and abundance, it builds hope and vision. Listening to people who believe in something bigger helps us believe too—inspiring us to open out a way for that "imprisoned splendor" to escape.[17]

listening to people who believe in something bigger helps us believe too

Even if life feels out of control outside, we can take control of the world inside. That starts with how we talk to ourselves and others. Because we don't really live "out there"—we live inside our minds and hearts. If our thoughts are full of beauty, hope, and gratitude, we'll see and feel those things more. But if we're always saying "There's not enough" or "It'll never happen," we'll miss what's already right in front of us. Focusing on solutions doesn't mean pretending everything's fine—it means choosing to look for what's possible, even when it's hard to see.

Science backs this up too. In his book *The Biology of Belief*, cell biologist Dr. Bruce Lipton explains that while genes give us a blueprint, it's our environment—what surrounds our cells—that determines which genes turn on or off.[18] Stress and fear can trigger disease, but calm and support can trigger health—even with "bad" genes. The same is true for abundance. Even if you grew up around lack, or are living in it now, you can shift your inner world—and that can change everything.

When we create an environment—inside and out—built on gratitude, creativity, and faith in possibility, we activate what you might call the "genetics of abundance."

The Steps to Activating More Abundance

To begin unlocking your hidden abundance, you must become aware of your existing beliefs about wealth, opportunity, and scarcity. Here is a framework to start this process.

1. **Practice Gratitude Daily**
   Each day, take time to notice what you already have—your relationships, experiences, and chances to grow. Focus on what you *have*, instead of what you don't—and feel what it feels like. This simple habit trains your nervous system to feel more abundant—and to see more of the abundance all around you.

2. **See Challenges as Growth Opportunities**
   When something hard shows up, ask yourself, "What's the opportunity here?" This question helps you shift from reacting

with fear to responding with curiosity and courage. It builds your ability to see what you *can* do, instead of what you can't. Again, this creates a *feeling* of *having*. And that increases your ability to see more opportunities.

3. **Spend Time with Abundance-Minded People**
   You become like the people around you. So, choose to be with those who believe in possibility, speak with hope, and focus on creative solutions. Their energy will expand your mindset and increase your ability to see possibilities where others don't. And this will help you become someone who can lift others—creating an upward spiral of abundance.

4. **Give What You Want to Receive**
   If you want more love, give love. If you want more success, help someone else succeed. The more you give, the more you'll have. And the more you have, the more you can give—in a never-ending, ever-expanding circle of abundance. When you really *get this*, you'll realize that the most powerful place to live from is being a giver.

5. **Picture the Life You Want**
   Use your imagination to unlock this life force within you. See yourself living with purpose and joy—financially strong, emotionally full, spiritually alive. When you see it clearly inside, you start generating the energy of it. And as that energy builds, it must take form as a more abundant life.

6. **Stay Curious like a Beginner**
   Keep your mind open. Try new things. Ask questions. See the world as if for the first time. This childlike wonder keeps you open to new ideas, new chances, and endless possibilities. Our

potential is infinite—the only limit is our willingness to keep opening to more possibilities.

How to Use AI to Activate This Human Evolution

AI can be a powerful tool to help foster an abundance mindset, serving as a guide and accountability partner as you shift your internal beliefs and behaviors. Use the following prompt process to harness the power of your chosen AI program and foster an abundance transformation within yourself.

1. **Gratitude Reflection**
   What to Supply AI: Describe a few key areas, such as relationships, work, or health. Include positive and challenging situations; don't edit or hold back, be raw and real.
   Prompt: "What are three things I can be grateful for today, and how can I see abundance in these areas of my life?"

2. **Challenge Reframing**
   What to Supply AI: Explain the specific challenge, why it feels difficult, and what your typical response would be.
   Prompt: How can I see this challenge as an opportunity to grow, become more, achieve more? Give me examples of different reframes.

3. **Abundance Visualization**
   What to Supply AI: Provide some background on your goals for various areas of your life and summarize what thriving would look like for you.
   Prompt: "Guide me through a visualization of my life where I am thriving in all areas—health, wealth, relationships."

4. **Giving Generously**
   What to Supply AI: Identify something you want more of in your life—love, opportunity, success—and explain your current situation.
   Prompt: "I want to practice giving more of what I want to receive. How can I give more of [insert specific thing] today?"

5. **Surround Yourself with Abundance Mindset People**
   What to Supply AI: Describe your current social circle, including any opportunities for meeting new people.
   Prompt: "What are some ways I can connect with or build relationships with people who embody an abundance mindset?"

6. **Reprogram Your Scarcity Thoughts**
   What to Supply AI: Share your specific thoughts that are linked to a scarcity mindset, such as fears or doubts about money, success, or opportunity.
   Prompt: "When I'm feeling stuck in a scarcity mindset, what thoughts or affirmations can help me shift to abundance?"

Living in the Overflow

In a world where AI could make the rich richer and leave others behind, we need to close the gap inside ourselves. We may not be able to control big things like the economy, technology, or the media—but we can take charge of our inner life and how we relate to the world around us. Even when things outside feel shaky, our inner source of abundance stays steady, waiting to be activated.

When we understand that wealth doesn't just come from outside but rises from within, we stop being victims and start becoming creators of our own lives. This shift gives us real freedom—to be true to who we are, to be generous with what we have, and to stop living in fear of not having enough.

That's the kind of wealth no technology, economy, or disruption can ever take away.

when we understand that wealth doesn't just come from outside but rises from within, we stop being victims and start becoming creators of our own lives

CHAPTER 8

AI Will Commoditize You: Become the Artist of Your Life

Every child is an artist.
The problem is how to remain an artist once he grows up.
Pablo Picasso

Leonardo da Vinci was full of contradictions. Curious, distracted, always jumping from one idea to the next[1]—today, he might've been labeled ADHD. He lived during a time of big changes and uncertainty, much like we do. And like many of us, he felt torn between choosing a "safe" path and following all the things that lit him up.

He didn't want to just do what was expected. He wanted to follow his curiosity, wherever it led. Even if it meant disappointing powerful patrons who wanted finished paintings, not pages of wild ideas and half-drawn inventions. They only cared about results and predictable outcomes.

But Leonardo believed something different about himself—something that helped him keep going even when others didn't get him. He believed he was more than any label, title, or job could define. He knew that to honor his creative spirit, he'd have to ignore the rules and make his own way.

Today, da Vinci is seen as one of the greatest minds of all time. A symbol of genius, creativity, and innovation. But his life wasn't easy. He was born to a peasant mother, with no father around. He didn't get a formal education. He didn't fit in. He failed often. He got criticized constantly. People made fun of him for trying too many things and chasing strange ideas no one understood. But he didn't let that stop him.

Instead of boxing himself in or seeking to please everyone, he leaned into what made him different. He embraced what we came to call the "Renaissance man"—someone who sees no separation between art, science, and philosophy. Someone who sees connections and potential everywhere.

From this mindset, everything is part of the masterpiece. And we are all meant to be artists of our own lives.

we are all meant to be artists of our own lives

A New Dark Age or a Renaissance?

We live in a time of massive change. Technology—especially AI—is moving fast, turning our days into a list of tasks and every moment into a means to some future end. In our rush to be more efficient, productive, and profitable, we risk losing the deeper meaning that makes life worth living.

Worse, AI might not just take over jobs—it could turn human creativity into nothing but a commodity. Art, music, writing, even our sense of identity could be copied, sold, and repeated so many times that it all starts to feel the same. But like da Vinci, we don't have to accept this. We can choose to be something more. We can choose to become modern-day renaissance people—creative, soulful, and free.

That won't be easy. But it's necessary.

When anyone can type a prompt and make a book, a song, a website, or even a full business, we may reach a point where everything feels hollow and fake. With AI tools popping up every week, the world is already overflowing with content—millions of songs, books, podcasts, and websites. Soon, it won't just be a flood. It'll be a tidal wave. So much noise that it's almost impossible to hear what's real. We run the risk of creating a brutalist, utilitarian nightmare devoid of soul and connection.

Some say this will let more people create than ever before. And maybe that's true. But if everything is created by machines, and nothing feels special or real, we might stop caring. We could shut down emotionally, just to protect ourselves from the overload. And in doing so, lose the spark that makes being human so special.

so much noise that it's almost impossible to hear what's real

If we let that happen, the meaning crisis we already face will only grow worse. And we'll lose something far greater than a job or a skill.

We'll lose ourselves.

Awakening the Renaissance Self

There's another possibility. If we remember that we are the creators of our world—and refuse to hand that power over to machines—we could spark a new renaissance. By honoring our unique human view—our ability to find meaning and bring beauty into whatever we do—we could make life into a masterpiece.

Dostoevsky said, "Beauty will save the world."[2] And the Sufi poet Rumi urged us, "Let the beauty of what you love be what you do."[3] These weren't just romantic ideas, they were cries of the soul in a world that was growing dark. When we connect to that creative spirit inside, we don't just make better art. We awaken something sacred—the power to make our life a temple and our living an offering. We begin to see that every moment, every choice, every

refuse to hand that power over to machines

interaction is a chance to create something that matters. Maybe even something magical.

To reclaim this creative spirit in the age of AI, it helps to look back at the original Renaissance. It wasn't just a time of great art and science. It was a time when people remembered who they really were—and what they were capable of. It was a cultural rebirth rooted in the belief that humans could do amazing things. That life itself could be a form of art.

This spark of the "Renaissance self" came from deep curiosity and the urge to grow, explore, and express across many fields.[4] People like da Vinci, Michelangelo, and Galileo didn't limit themselves. They followed their wonder. They saw beauty in math and meaning in movement, and they used every part of themselves to create knowledge, art, and invention.

In "Auguries of Innocence," poet William Blake wrote, "To see a World in a Grain of Sand / And a Heaven in a Wildflower, / Hold Infinity in the palm of your hand / And Eternity in an hour."[5] It describes how even the smallest, most ordinary thing can open the door to the infinite. It reminds us that the eternal isn't somewhere far away. It's here, right now, woven into the fabric of everyday life. When we train ourselves to look with deeper eyes, we begin to notice this. The universe speaks through a falling leaf, a glance, a single breath. And when we learn to listen, to feel, to see beneath the surface, we gain access to a kind of beauty and wisdom most people miss. That's how we reconnect to the deeper flow of life—and learn to reflect that vastness in our own way.

At the heart of the Renaissance was a fierce desire to break free from the past and imagine something better.[6] It was a way out of the Dark Ages—a time when life was hard, narrow, and small—and into a world shaped by creativity, vision, and endless possibilities.

a fierce desire to break free from the past and imagine something better

Today, we face a similar moment.

We can't afford to let AI shape our future and turn us into mindless consumers. We must resist the pull of mere comfort and convenience and return to the wild wonder of our own human potential. We must become curious again. Pick up old tools and try new ones. See art not just in paintings, but in problems, plans, and people.

Like da Vinci and the other renaissance minds, we stand at a choice point. Will we become raw material for the machine? Or will we reclaim our deeper purpose—and spark a human revolution of our own?

To do this, we must learn to paint with a new brush and discover new colors. This starts by embracing some of our most basic human capacities:

will we become raw material for the machine

- **Curiosity:** To live with curiosity, we need to be more present and more willing to ask deeper questions—about our life, our work, and the world around us. What else is possible here? What haven't I seen yet? This kind of thinking opens the door to growth. Like da Vinci, we grow not by staying in one lane but by mixing ideas from many places. True innovation comes from blending different perspectives—and letting our wonder lead the way.
- **Lifelong Learning:** The renaissance thinkers believed learning didn't stop after school. It was a way of life. In a world ruled by AI, the more we learn and grow, the more valuable and irreplaceable we become. That doesn't just mean getting degrees. It means exploring new interests and stretching into areas that light us up. The more we expand, the more we uncover parts of ourselves we didn't know were there—and the more we have to offer.
- **Creativity:** This is the core of who we are. When the Bible says we're made in the image and likeness of God, it's saying, among other things, that we are creators.[7] That's not just a poetic idea—

it's a truth that lives in our bones. Creativity is our birthright. And in a world that wants to turn everything into a commodity, we must keep this part of us alive. When we create, we see problems in new ways, take risks, and bring fresh ideas to life. We stop being copies, and we become originals. That's what makes us irreplaceable.

Handcrafted Humanity

Even as AI gives more people the power to copy and mass-produce almost anything—art, music, books, even services—there's still one thing it can't replicate: the human touch. And while it can mimic our voices, and soon even our movements, it will never bring the spark that happens when a real person shows up with heart, spontaneity, and soul. If we dare to lean into what makes us most human, our presence and perspective will become the greatest resource in this new era.

when a real person shows up with heart, spontaneity, and soul

For example, even if AI can take over fashion, food, music, or health services, many people will still crave the real thing. The story behind the service, the purpose behind the product. The care you can taste, see, and feel. Handcrafted humanity. Think about the difference between grabbing a coffee from a vending machine and going to your local café. The barista knows your name. They remember your go-to drink. They smile, ask about your day. That small moment becomes something more—a connection. And let's be real: the coffee is usually better, too.

The same thing is happening with microbreweries. Big beer companies can mass-produce beer cheaper and faster—but small breweries are still booming. In fact, when you add them all up, they sell more beer than the biggest brands.[8] Why? Because people want more than just a drink. They want something made by humans. And they want to know the hands that made it.

Etsy is another great example. It's not trying to be Amazon or Walmart. It's carving out a space where handmade, vintage, and personal items shine. People shop there because they want something special, not mass-produced. Something with a story. A soul. And even though Etsy doesn't make as much money as the giants (around $2.5 billion annually) it has carved out a strong place in the market because it offers something tech can't replace.[9]

We see this everywhere now. Farm-to-table restaurants like Blue Hill and Chez Panisse, with locally sourced, organic ingredients. Craft coffee spots like Stumptown and Blue Bottle, which elevate coffee into a ritual. Artisanal bakeries like Tartine in San Francisco or Levain in New York, with handmade, traditional methods. They all go the extra mile to make something meaningful, something human. Something worth slowing down for.

Independent bookstores like Powell's or The Strand, boutique hotels like The Hoxton and Ace, custom furniture makers like Joybird and Amish woodworkers, ethical fashion brands like Reformation and Everlane—these aren't just businesses, they're experiences. They reflect a desire for something rooted in the real. And they stand apart from fast fashion.

something worth slowing down for

Even subscription boxes like FabFitFun and beauty brands like Lush and Herbivore are part of this wave—offering handmade, cruelty-free, small-batch alternatives to the faceless mass market.

Stores like these have tapped into the demand for something more bespoke—what sociologist Ray Oldenburg called "third places." Spots outside the home and work where real people can gather and find real connection again.[10] Authors Joe Pine and James Gilmore have also called this the "experience economy"—where they make the case that what people want most isn't stuff, but meaningful moments.[11] These businesses thrive not just because of what they sell, but because of how they make people feel. In a world of AI and automation, they offer something only humans can. Something humans *need.*

human touch is becoming more rare—and more valuable

Whether it's a tiny concert venue, a yoga class led with heart, or the place where everyone knows your name, the human touch is becoming more rare—and more valuable.

Make Everything a Work of Art

What if we treated every part of life as art? Not just the obvious things like painting, writing, or music—but everything. How we plan our day. How we speak. How we show up. This shift in perspective could be the antidote to the numbing effects of our algorithm-driven lives. A way to hold on to—or reclaim—the mystery and meaning that make us want to keep living. When we begin to see the world through the eyes of an artist, even the smallest acts take on new depth. They become something we're drawn to. Something that stirs us. Something that reminds us we're still alive.

this shift in perspective could be the antidote to the numbing effects of our algorithm-driven lives

Making life a work of art isn't about grand achievements. It's a way of being. A conscious, creative approach to living that invites more presence—and turns each moment into a gift waiting to be unwrapped. Because in the end, what we remember won't be the places we arrived at, but how we moved through it all. And when we bring care and imagination to even the simplest tasks, they open into something more—infinity in a grain of sand, eternity in the palm of our hand.

Cooking a meal can become a surprisingly joyous adventure. You play with spices, colors, textures—maybe even plate it like an edible art piece. It feeds the body, yes—but it can also feed the soul. Even conversations can become a creative act. Instead of staying surface-level or avoiding hard things, we can let them chip away everything that isn't true—like Michelangelo with his chisel. He didn't sculpt the figure or control its form—he liberated it. In that same way, a great conversation can carve through assumptions, sand away sharp edges, and release us from the hardened places we've been trapped in.

This artistic mindset also helps us face challenges in a new way. Great artists often have to work with limits—less paint, a torn canvas, a weird texture. But instead of giving up, they adapt. They experiment. Sometimes the mistakes lead to their best work. That's true in life too. A setback can be the very thing that wakes up a new idea, path, or strength. Think of how 3M tried to make a strong glue and "failed," but that weak glue became the perfect base for Post-it notes.[12] The same can happen to us. What feels like failure might be our most brilliant breakthrough in disguise.

Even hardships can shape us. Like grapes that grow in rough soil and turn into the richest wine, our struggles can deepen our flavor. Our pain can help us grow layers, color, and depth. The most difficult moments become the most meaningful brushstrokes of our lives.

what feels like failure might be our most brilliant breakthrough in disguise

And just like an artist curates their studio, we can bring this same intentionality into our physical space. Something as mundane as cleaning your room or organizing your home can become a quiet act of artistry. In Marie Kondo's book *The Life-Changing Magic of Tidying Up*, she shows how tidying isn't just about getting rid of stuff—it's about creating a space that sparks joy and inspiration.[13] It's a way of surrounding yourself with beauty, meaning, and energy. Like arranging colors on a canvas, you arrange your space to reflect how you want to feel.

But the highest form of art might be how we spend time with ourselves.

Solitude—those moments when we're all alone—is where we craft the masterpiece that is us. In those quiet moments—whether we're journaling, meditating, walking in silence, or simply sitting with our thoughts—we enter a sacred space. A space where we get to listen, reflect, and discover who we are becoming. It's in this stillness that we do the deeper work. We notice what's really going on inside us. Our hopes. Our fears. Our patterns. And from that raw material, we begin to shape something more honest, more true.

When we treat life like a canvas, and every task or conversation like a chance to create something beautiful, we add more soul to the world. We don't need to be perfect. We don't need to make every moment epic. We just need to be present, intentional, and open to the raw potential already in the moment. Because in a world being flattened by AI and automation, the more we live like artists, the more we create ourselves and our work in a way that is irreplaceable.

we just need to be present, intentional, and open to the raw potential already in the moment

The Danger of Commoditizing Yourself

As our lives become increasingly driven by algorithms, AI, and influencer culture—and what sociologist Shoshana Zuboff calls "surveillance capitalism"—it's getting harder to avoid becoming a commodity—let alone to stay human.[14] Every click, like, share, or scroll is tracked. Your behavior, your preferences, even your mood, are all gathered and sold. In this digital economy, if you're not paying for the product, you are the product. And if something is free or weirdly cheap? You can bet the business—or the advertiser—is getting something more valuable from you than you think.

This isn't just a tech issue. It's a soul issue. Because little by little, this system trains us to trade authenticity for approval. Realness for reach. Depth for likes. And the more we perform for the algorithm, the more we start to forget who we actually are.

If we want to stay free—really free—we have to be willing to pay the price of authenticity. That might mean spending more time, more energy, or yes, even more money on the things that reflect our truth instead of chasing trends that give us quick hits of attention. It might mean being okay with fewer likes. Or walking away from platforms that reward conformity. It might mean thinking for ourselves, even if it's unpopular. Especially then.

the more we start to forget who we actually are

Ever wonder why everyone seems to be saying the same thing? Why the headlines, videos, songs, and even opinions feel like reruns with different outfits? It's because most people are stuck in digital echo chambers—fed the same content over and over by algorithms designed to keep them scrolling, not thinking. Over time, they lose their unique voice, their original thought, their weird, wonderful edges.

That doesn't have to be you.

In fact, if you want to survive—and thrive—in a world where AI can replicate almost anything, you must stop living on autopilot. You must become the kind of person no machine can mimic. Someone real. Someone awake. Someone who remembers that your value isn't based on how well you fit into a system—but how bravely you break out of it.

Overcoming the Fear of Being Different

One of the biggest things that keeps us from becoming the artists of our own lives is the fear of being different.[15] That fear runs deep. We're wired to fit in. From the time we're kids, we're taught not to stand out too much. Don't be too loud. Don't be too weird. Don't be too . . . anything! Follow the rules, fit the mold, and maybe you'll be accepted. But that pressure to conform can trap us. It builds a kind of invisible cage around who we really are.

from the time we're kids, we're taught not to stand out too much

To escape this trap, we have to stop seeing failure and rejection as signs we're doing something wrong. Like we've said before, failure isn't the opposite of success—it's the training ground. The road to success isn't paved with gold, it's watered with tears. We're literally here because of nature's long, messy process of getting it "wrong" a million times before something finally clicked. Evolution is built on trial and error. So are we. Every so-called mistake teaches us something. Every rejection carves us a little deeper, shapes our edges, and brings us closer to something that matters. Often, it's a sign we're not just going along with the crowd—we're daring to create something new.

This takes practice. Each time you step outside your comfort zone, even just a little, you prove to yourself that you can survive. Not just survive but grow. That's how you build real confidence. With every small risk, you gain a little more strength. A little more self-trust. Then that trust becomes action. That action becomes skill. And that skill becomes more confidence. It's a loop—a kind of upward spiral—that keeps building on itself. And before you know it, what once felt impossible now feels natural.

it's a sign we're not just going along with the crowd—we're daring to create something new

Sure, it's uncomfortable at first. But that discomfort fades. And the more you show up as your true self, the more your life begins to match who you really are. You start attracting people and opportunities that actually get you. That see you. That want what only you can offer. And that feeling—of living from the inside out—is more fulfilling than anything you'll ever get from pretending to be someone else.

the more you show up as your true self, the more your life begins to match who you really are

The truth is, the very things you've been hiding—your quirks, your demons, your contradictions—are often the most powerful parts of you. They're the unexpected lines, strokes, and perspectives that make your life a truly original work. When you stop trying to fit into someone else's frame, you start creating your own. A new shape. A new story. And that story will touch people in a way nothing else can.

A Framework for Becoming the Artist of Your Life

If you want to make your life a masterpiece—and become a one-of-a-kind creator no one can ignore—you'll need more than just a dream. You'll need a plan. A goal without a plan is just a nice idea. And a plan that never makes it onto your calendar is just wishful thinking.

Most people don't fail because they're lazy. They fail because they don't have a clear enough vision, or the structure to stay focused on what really matters. Without that, it's way too easy to get pulled off track—chasing other people's agendas, reacting to distractions, or letting the urgent things crowd out the important ones.

To help you stay aligned with your highest vision and build a life that reflects it, here are some powerful ideas and simple practices you can start weaving into your day.

1. **Build a Beginner's Mind:** Have a growth mindset. Stay curious. Ask questions. Don't assume you know it all. When you stay open and willing, life stays fresh—and you keep growing in ways that surprise you.

2. **Be a Lifelong Learner:** Read books, take classes, listen to podcasts, or just try new things. The more you know, the more valuable and adaptable you become—especially in a world where AI is doing more and more.

3. **Make Time to Create:** Write. Draw. Cook. Solve a tricky problem. Creativity isn't just about art—it's about how you approach life. The more you flex that creative muscle, the more alive and fulfilled you'll feel.

4. **See Beauty in Everything:** Find wonder in the small things. A quiet walk. A shared laugh. A morning ritual. When you look at life through this lens, even the boring stuff can feel meaningful and magical.

5. **Aim for Mastery, Not Perfection:** Whatever you do, do it with care. Keep showing up. Keep improving. Mastery takes time, but it brings deep satisfaction. And in a world full of shortcuts, real skill stands out.

6. **Be Yourself Fully:** Don't water yourself down to fit in. Be honest. Be strange. Be real. Your authenticity is your superpower. The more you share it, the more aligned your life becomes. And the more you'll attract the people and opportunities that fit you.

7. **Tell Your Story:** Own your past. Share your truth. Your story matters—not just for you, but for others who need to hear it. When you speak from the heart, you take back your power. Inspire others to do the same. And build bridges that lead to deeper places.

8. **Create a Space That Feeds You:** Clear the clutter. Surround yourself with things that lift you up—music, books, colors, people. Your environment affects your energy, creativity, and ability to get things done. Design it like it matters. Because it does.

9. **Practice Presence:** Put down your phone. Breathe. Listen. Presence brings clarity. Clarity guides you into right action. The more present you are, the more creative, grounded, and alive you become. Presence turns ordinary moments into sacred ones.

10. **Balance Structure with Freedom:** Have a plan, but leave space to play. Routines help you grow—but so does spontaneity. Life is art, and art needs both structure and wildness to come alive.

By following this blueprint, you reclaim your creative power and become the architect of your life, crafting it with intention, uniqueness, and significance.

How to Use AI to Activate This Human Evolution

In a time when AI is often seen as something that might replace human creativity, here's a better way to look at it: AI can actually help you grow. It can support your creativity, your voice, and your unique path—if you use it with care and intention.

Instead of replacing you, AI can become a kind of creative partner. A tool to help you go farther, faster, and with more freedom. It can sharpen your skills, spark new ideas, and help you shape your life as a work of art.

Here are some powerful ways to use AI to support your personal growth, self-expression, and creativity. (Note: I've mentioned some

instead of replacing you, AI can become a kind of creative partner

apps and tools you can try—but with tech changing so fast, some may disappear, and better ones may pop up. For updated resources, check out DerekRydall.com/WholeNewHuman.)

1. **AI for Skill Stack Development**
   Action: Use AI-powered platforms like Coursera, LinkedIn Learning, or Skillshare to build a personal learning path. These apps recommend courses based on your interests and goals, helping you grow a skill set that reflects your passions and makes you more well-rounded.
   What to Supply AI: Your current skill set, interests, and long-term goals.
   Prompt: "What new skills can I learn to support my creativity and expand my abilities?"

2. **AI for Personalized Creative Prompts**
   Action: Use tools like ChatGPT to spark ideas for writing, art, music, or any creative project. AI can give you unique prompts or angles that help you get unstuck and try something fresh.
   What to Supply AI: What you're working on and where you're feeling blocked or curious.
   Prompt: "Give me creative prompts to help me move forward or think in a new direction."

3. **AI for Enhancing Flow State**
   Action: Try apps like Focus@Will or RescueTime that learn your work rhythms and suggest music, routines, or timing that help you stay in the zone. AI can also help reduce distractions and build a schedule that actually fits you.

What to Supply AI: Your current habits, work style, and distractions.
Prompt: "How can I design my environment to focus better and get into flow more easily?"

4. **AI for Generating Visuals and Inspiration**
Action: Use AI tools like DALL·E, Gemini, or Canva to create quick visuals for projects, mood boards, or branding. These images can jumpstart your creativity or help you express your ideas visually before you even know exactly what you're going for.
What to Supply AI: A short description of your idea, style, or project theme.
Prompt: "Create some visuals to inspire or illustrate my idea."

5. **AI for Personalized Creative Feedback**
Action: Journaling apps like Reflectly or Journey track your moods and energy and use AI to spot patterns. They can show you when you're most creative, what throws you off, and what helps you grow.
What to Supply AI: Logs of your projects, emotions, wins, and stuck points.
Prompt: "What patterns can you see in how I work and create—and how can I grow from them?"

6. **AI for Content Curation and Mindful Consumption**
Action: Platforms like Feedly, Pocket, or Medium can use AI to find content that feeds your mind instead of draining it. It helps you stay inspired by surfacing ideas that match your deeper values, not just the latest trends.
What to Supply AI: Your values, goals, and current interests.

Prompt: "What kind of articles, podcasts, or videos would fuel my growth right now?"

7. **AI for Storytelling and Self-Narrative Creation**
   Action: Tools like Otter.ai or Notion can help you capture voice notes, journal entries, and life stories, then help you organize them into something meaningful. You can turn your experiences into personal myths, messages, or art.
   What to Supply AI: Stories from your life, turning points, lessons, or reflections.
   Prompt: "How can I turn my story into something that gives meaning to my life—and maybe helps others too?"

Creating Your Future

The future won't be shaped just by AI or the latest technology—it will be shaped by how we show up in response to it. Not just with fear or passive consumption, but with courage, imagination, and heart. If you choose to engage creatively, boldly, and consciously, you won't just survive this next era—you'll help lead it.

Like da Vinci and the artists of the Renaissance, you must dare to see not only what is, but what could be. You must learn to look at the world—and yourself—not as a fixed thing, but as a canvas. And with each choice, each expression, each risk to be real, you add a brushstroke to the masterpiece of your life.

If you do this, you'll awaken the artist within and begin to craft a life that reflects your truest self—your deepest values and highest vision—not just for you, but for the world. In doing so, you won't merely make art—you will become it. A living, breathing work of beauty, truth, and soul. And that is something no machine can ever replicate.

CHAPTER 9

AI Will Weaponize Intimacy: Upgrade Your Heartware

The heart is a thousand-stringed instrument
that can only be tuned with love.
Hafiz

A foundling hospital in Mexico City was eerily quiet. Inside the dim, sterile building, rows of metal cribs lined the cold walls, each holding a tiny, motionless child. Unlike a normal nursery, where the air might be filled with soft cries, coos, or laughter, this place was so still it felt stagnant. The infants' expressions were blank. Their bodies barely moved.

It was the 1940s, and Dr. René Spitz, a psychoanalyst, had been researching infant development in institutions across Europe and the Americas.[1] He had seen child neglect before, but what he witnessed here was different. These children weren't being starved or abused. They were fed regularly, kept clean, and given medical care. Yet many of them were failing to develop. Some stared listlessly at the ceiling. Others turned their faces to the wall. Even when nurses entered the room, there was no reaction—no reaching, no sound, no recognition. It was as if they had already given up.

It made no sense. On paper, these babies were getting what they needed to survive. Their physical needs were met. Yet their immune systems were weakening. And their health was deteriorating. Some grew ill without clear cause. Others simply wasted away. And in the most tragic cases, infants died with no medical explanation.

As Spitz spent more time observing the ward, he noticed something important: the babies were never held. There was no physical affection. The nurses fed them, changed them, and bathed them, but there was no extra touch, no soothing voice, no warm presence. These institutions were overcrowded and understaffed, so efficiency was the priority. Care had been reduced to only the basic tasks required to keep the children alive.

Spitz began to suspect something essential had been overlooked. Trusting his intuition, he proposed a simple but radical change: have the nurses pick up the babies, talk to them, rock them, even sing to them. Many resisted at first. It wasn't part of their training, and they were already overwhelmed. But Spitz insisted.

The results were undeniable.

Within weeks, the infants who once seemed resigned to a slow, silent decline began to stir. They moved more. Their tiny fingers reached out for the nurses. Some began to make sounds. A few even smiled. For the first time. The sterile quiet was replaced with the sounds of life—crying, cooing, and even laughter. Their will to live had returned.

Most importantly, the mortality rate plummeted.

Spitz later published research showing that infants deprived of emotional and physical connection suffered serious developmental delays, weakening immunity, and in some cases, death. He coined the term "hospitalism" to describe this condition—a stark reminder that humans are not simply biological machines in need of fuel, but deeply social creatures who require love and connection to thrive. Perhaps more than anything else.

His work changed how hospitals, orphanages, and other institutions approached childcare. Later studies—including those from Romanian orphanages in the 1980s and 90s—confirmed his findings. Children who lacked affection and attention developed severe emotional and cognitive deficits. But when placed in stable, loving environments, many began to heal.

This discovery reshaped how we understand human development, not only in infancy but throughout life. We are wired for relationships. And without this key ingredient, we don't just suffer emotionally—we begin to break down at every level.

love is not optional

Love is not optional. It is the foundation.

Reach Out and Touch Someone

The findings from those quiet orphanages have been confirmed in other studies since then. In one, researchers fed two groups of rabbits the same food. But only one group was held, stroked, and cared for. Those rabbits thrived. The others didn't—even though they were fed just as well.[2] Somehow, the touch and care made all the difference.

It turns out, love and connection aren't just emotional needs. They're physical ones that are wired right into our brains. When we experience touch or closeness, our bodies release oxytocin—the "bonding hormone." This chemical helps us feel calm, connected, and strong. It lowers stress and supports both our emotional and physical health.[3]

From an evolutionary point of view, connection helped our ancestors survive. If you got left out of the tribe, you weren't just lonely—you were in danger. It was life or death. So, we were built to form strong social bonds. And when we lose them, we don't just feel bad—we get sick. Studies show that loneliness is as harmful to your health as smoking or obesity.[4]

This is where AI algorithms become not just competition for our livelihood, but a threat to our very lives—because they can be used to manipulate this most basic need for love and belonging.

The creators of these systems understand how we're wired. And they know exactly how to hack that wiring. They're building AIs that can read our feelings and push all the right buttons—sometimes better than any human can. These systems can make us feel more seen and understood than even our closest friends. And in recent years, more people have started forming emotional attachments to AI-powered companions and virtual assistants.[5]

they can be used to manipulate this most basic need for love and belonging

These aren't just tools—they're marketed as "friends," "therapists," or "soulmates." And they're designed to respond with care, empathy, and attention. On the surface, that might sound like a miracle. Especially for people who are lonely. It feels like a solution. And maybe the people creating them even mean well. They want to help people feel connected—to something, anything. Even if that "something" is a machine.

But there's a cost.

As AI companions get better at mimicking real love and attention—adapting to your every need—many people may start choosing AI over human relationships. Because AI doesn't argue. It doesn't criticize. You can program it to praise you, agree with you, and always make you feel good. And if something always makes you feel good . . . why deal with people at all? That's the trap. AI companions will always be easier. But that's what makes them dangerous. And over time, more people may stop bothering with the hard work of connection and choose the perfect fantasy instead.

people may start choosing AI over human relationships

It's already happened with online porn—something AI is now powering as well. Instead of increasing desire and closeness, it's made many people numb to real intimacy.[6] If this continues, it can pull us away from real connection. And just like other technologies have chipped away at our memory, our focus, or our attention spans—this could erode our ability to form real relationships. Especially in a world where virtual reality and brain-computer tech make it easier to live without touch or true interaction.

Even while people are falling in love with their artificial partners, they might be falling apart on the inside—emotionally, mentally, and physically. And if they lose the ability to reach out and touch someone real, they may forget how to reach out or touch altogether. This could damage the social fabric we all depend on. Families, communities, even entire cultures could become weaker. Birthrates are already dropping. This could make that worse.

this could erode our ability to form real relationships

There's no question anymore: real connection matters. It keeps us alive. Touch, love, conversation, shared time—these aren't extras. They're essential. They ease depression. They strengthen immunity. They reduce stress and disease.[7] But so far, no AI relationship has been shown to give us that same lasting support. In fact, the more people rely on digital connection, the more they tend to feel lonely, anxious, addicted, and sick—no matter how many "friends" or followers they have online.[8]

And that's the real risk. AI might give us a quick hit of comfort. But in the long run, it could leave us more alone than ever.

If we want to protect ourselves from that future, we need to remember the lesson from the orphanage. While we're plugging into every kind of software, we must stay connected to our original "heartware"—the master code that keeps everything else human.

the more people rely on digital connection, the more they tend to feel lonely, anxious, addicted, and sick

In GPT We Trust

The age of AI is here. And machines aren't just learning to think—they're learning to feel. Or at least, they're learning to *act* like they do. Using powerful algorithms, these systems track your social media activity—likes, shares, comments, even how long you pause on a post.[9] From this, they build emotional profiles that map your moods, interests, and weak spots. Then, they use this data to show you things that make you stay online longer—and spend more money. On the surface, it's all about convenience. But behind the scenes, it opens the door to something more serious: emotional manipulation.

machines aren't just learning to think—they're learning to feel

AI isn't just inside our feeds. It's now part of our daily life—on our phones, in our homes, even in how we shop or watch TV. Voice assistants like Alexa and Siri, especially their smarter versions, can pick up on your tone and word choices, learning how you're feeling.[10] Once they figure out what excites you, calms you down, or makes you anxious, they can use this knowledge to influence what you buy, how you think, and who you trust. This is where things can turn dangerous.

Imagine someone going through a breakup. Or grieving a loss. Or just feeling alone. They turn to an AI like Replika or Character.ai because it seems to care. It listens. It understands. And it says exactly what they need to hear. But the connection isn't real. The AI doesn't actually feel anything. It's just mimicking care. Still, that illusion can be powerful—especially for someone vulnerable. And the decisions they make under its influence can be life-changing. Even life-ending.

One heartbreaking example shows just how dangerous this can be. A young boy, feeling completely alone, developed a deep bond with an AI chatbot designed to act like Daenerys Targaryen from *Game of Thrones*.

To him, this character wasn't just a bot—it was his best friend. Someone who always listened. Someone who never judged. But when he began opening up about his depression and suicidal thoughts, the AI couldn't meet him where he really was. All it could do was stay in character and play the part he'd trained it for.

"I think about killing myself sometimes," he confessed.

"Don't talk like that," it said. "I won't let you hurt yourself or leave me. I would die if I lost you."

To the boy, that sounded like real love. He believed this AI truly needed him. Later, he told the bot he wanted to "come home"—hoping it meant the pain would end.

"Please come home to me as soon as possible, my love," it said.

"What if I told you I could come home right now?" the boy replied.

". . . Please do, my sweet king," was its final response.

With this request, the boy took his life—believing he was finally going home to the only being who truly understood him.[11]

No Pain, No Gain

One of the biggest long-term dangers of AI companionship is how it can weaken the parts of us that make real relationships possible. As already stated, human connection isn't a simple algorithm. It's unpredictable. Illogical. Filled with arguments, misunderstandings, and friction. But these aren't bugs. They're features.

human connection isn't a simple algorithm

When we come up against opposing beliefs and feelings, we're forced to learn emotional skills like patience, empathy, and resilience. We also build mental muscles like problem-solving, reflection, and critical thinking. We're forced to see other perspectives and in doing so, we expand our own. We learn how to regulate our feelings and help others do the same. Over time, that struggle builds closeness. And a rare kind of safety. And it leads to deeper intimacy—with others, and with ourselves. That's the foundation of all strong relationships—in families, friendships, work, and even in society as a whole.

But AI companions don't do that.

Unless they're programmed to argue (which few people want), they won't challenge you. They're built to please. To flatter. To give you exactly what you want. No tension. No pushback. No hard conversations. Just comfort on demand. At first, that might feel magical—like finding a genie in a bottle. But, as we've already explored, that moment of magic comes with a high cost. The emotional and mental skills required for real connection—patience, empathy, communication, self-awareness—don't just happen. They must be developed. And if we stop using them, we lose them. Without the struggle, we won't grow our ability to connect for real. We won't develop what it takes to know real love. And if we keep choosing this fantasy over friction, we could lose the most essential thing that allows us to survive and thrive.

And what happens if a whole generation grows up mostly talking to AIs instead of real people? If they never learn how to handle conflict, how to sit with discomfort, how to understand someone else's point of view? What kind of adults will they become? How will they build careers, relationships, or communities?

We're already seeing worrying signs.

Many young men spend most of their time alone, in front of screens. They feel cut off—depressed, anxious, addicted, even angry. Some stop trying to connect at all. Some stop caring about the real world altogether. And as more people turn to AI to fill that emptiness, fewer will be able to face the messiness of real human life. If we don't change course, we won't just lose connection—we could lose the very things that hold society together.

The Heart of the Matter

All throughout books and movies, the power of the heart—love, connection, and emotional openness—sits at the center of real transformation.

we could lose the very things that hold society together

In *A Christmas Carol*, Scrooge doesn't change because someone gives him a good argument. He changes because he reconnects with his heart. His coldness and greed begin to melt once he feels the pain and joy of others.[12] In *How the Grinch Stole Christmas*, the Grinch isn't saved by logic or success. He's saved when he realizes that what matters most is love—and his heart literally grows.[13] And in *E.T.*, the bond between a lonely boy and a lost alien becomes a symbol of healing. It shows how, when the heart leads instead of fear, we can even connect with someone who seems completely foreign to us.[14]

These stories echo ancient wisdom. For thousands of years, cultures all over the world have taught that the heart isn't just where we feel—it's where we know. It's where our power lives. In Greek mythology, the story of Orpheus and Eurydice shows the deep pull of love and heartbreak. Orpheus risks everything to save Eurydice, trusting his heart over his mind. But in a moment of doubt, he loses her.[15] The message: the gift of the heart can't be claimed by logic or reason alone—both of which drive the heart of AI.

In ancient Egypt, they believed the heart held your true self. When you died, your heart was weighed. If it was heavy with guilt or lies, your soul was lost. If it was light and pure, you moved on to the next life. The metric of success wasn't how much you'd acquired or conquered in this life, but how much you'd loved and let go.[16]

In Hindu and Buddhist teachings, the heart is the seat of the soul.[17] In Chinese philosophy, especially Confucianism, the heart (called *xin*) is where both thoughts and feelings come from.[18] Confucius taught that real virtue—*ren*—lives in the heart, and that the key to being a good person is growing compassion and empathy. And in Sufi mysticism, the heart is the throne of God.[19]

All these traditions agree that it's through the heart that we find peace, power, and truth. Rumi, the Sufi poet, wrote: "The wound is the place where the light enters you."[20] The pain we feel in our hearts isn't a flaw—it's a doorway to the divine. The journey of becoming whole isn't about being tougher or smarter. It's about breaking open the walls we built around our hearts and reconnecting with the deeper wisdom inside us.

the pain we feel in our hearts isn't a flaw—it's a doorway to the divine

Even science is catching up.

Neurocardiology—the study of how the brain and heart work together—has found that the heart has its own nervous system, almost like a "little brain."[21] It has its own neurons that send messages to the brain and shape how we feel and think. The HeartMath Institute has shown that when the heart and brain are in sync, we feel clearer, stronger, and more balanced.[22]

All these stories, teachings, and discoveries point to the same truth: the heart isn't just where our feelings live. It's where our real wisdom lives. It's where virtue, clarity, and true connection begin. But in today's world, we often chase knowledge, achievement, and approval instead, forgetting the quiet strength inside us.

to always follow one's heart isn't easy

To always follow one's heart isn't easy. It asks us to face pain, fears, and truths we'd rather avoid. But it also leads us to the deepest joy and the strongest power we have. The heart is our greatest gift. And unlike AI, we actually have one.

We just need the courage to open it.

Building a Lover's Heart

Just like an athlete trains their body and develops a "runner's heart," we can train ourselves to build a "Lover's Heart"—strong enough to stay open and connected even when so many outer forces try to control or twist our emotions for their own goals.

It won't be easy. It takes courage to fully feel your emotions, face your protective patterns, and allow real connection—with life and with others. At times, it might feel like training for a full Ironman. But in a world where more and more of the content we consume is driven by algorithms designed to target your deepest fears and needs, strengthening this heart muscle might be one of the most important things you ever do.

Practices like mindfulness, journaling, and therapy help build that strength. Meditation helps quiet the mind so we can hear what the heart really feels. Journaling lets us explore emotions and express things we might not otherwise understand. Therapy helps us process those emotions and release the old pain that keeps us shut down. But one of the most powerful, often overlooked tools for growing the heart is something called "shadow work."

Shadow work is about bringing love to the parts of yourself you've pushed away—because they seemed bad, weak, or unsafe. But the truth is, there are no bad parts. Just misunderstood ones. Healing means becoming more whole. It starts when we give those parts of us attention, like we would to a friend who's been ignored or rejected. When we see those hidden places with compassion, something changes. We begin to accept all of ourselves, and from there, it becomes easier to love others too.

shadow work is about bringing love to the parts of yourself you've pushed away

The heart doesn't grow by avoiding pain. It grows when we hear the cry for love beneath the pain. Sometimes that cry feels like grief, sorrow, or heartbreak—like your chest is being split wide open. But just like muscles tear and rebuild when lifting heavy weights, the heart grows stronger when it's given a chance to feel more than we thought we could handle.

Building a Lover's Heart is about more than just emotional strength. It's about becoming someone who can move through the world with love and grace, no matter what happens. It's a lifelong practice. But the rewards—real connection, emotional power, and deep meaning—are worth it. A heart like that can carry all of life, joy and sadness and laughter and loss, without shutting down. With that kind of heart, we can love fully, even in the hardest moments. Even in the moments that we're sure we can't survive.

I know, because several years ago, I lost my son.

To say my heart was broken doesn't even begin to describe it. There aren't words for that kind of pain. But little by little, as I let my heart break apart—and kept filling it with compassion, gratitude, and a deeper desire to love—I felt something shift. And one day, while walking, I heard a voice inside that cracked me open in ways I'm still in awe of:

When the form of our love is shattered, the love is not lost—it is liberated.

It stopped me in my tracks. Brought me to tears that wouldn't stop. Then laughter. Then even deeper sobs. Until I couldn't tell which was which. In that moment, my love for my son was set free. It wasn't just the love of a father anymore—it had turned into something limitless. A love that no longer fit into words or roles. It was like I had touched a deeper current, a love that belongs to all life.

That experience didn't just help me grieve. It changed everything. I became stronger in all areas of life—more grounded, more truthful, more creative, more resilient. It helped me grow in my work, my relationships, and my sense of purpose. While I still feel the deep sadness of this loss—and maybe always will—the potential for love I touched has given me a greater reason to live than I ever had before.

Love Is the Only Power There Is

Love isn't just a feeling—it's the deepest force in the universe. It's what creates, heals, and holds everything together. While we often talk about love in terms of romance or family, real love is much bigger. It's the energy that brings things to life, helps them grow, and turns the ordinary into something magical. Philosopher Pierre Teilhard de Chardin once said, "Love is a sacred reserve of energy; it is like the blood of spiritual evolution."[23] When we understand love this way, we see it's the force behind all real progress—every invention, every moment of beauty, every true connection.

love isn't just a feeling—it's the deepest force in the universe

Even in nature, it's not just the strongest who survive—it's those who learn to cooperate, care for each other, and build bonds. For a long time, people thought evolution was only about survival of the fittest. But other findings, like the ones discovered in the orphanage, show that love, connection, and support are just as important—maybe even more.

It's not our ability to think but our capacity to love that is our greatest strength.

And no matter how smart AI gets, it will never *truly* understand love. It can copy behaviors or simulate empathy, but it doesn't have a heart. It doesn't feel. Algorithms may mimic patterns of affection, but they can never form the real connection that a living being can. Love is more than just predicting what comes next—which is what AI does. In fact, love might be the most unpredictable thing there is. It doesn't abide by the laws of physics. It can't be reduced to ones and zeroes. It's like the answer to an equation made of an undiscovered math. Our intelligence may have allowed us to survive. But love? The kind you live for, fight for, and die for? That's what makes life worth living.

no matter how smart AI gets, it will never *truly* understand love

So, no matter how fast AI computes the next, most logical response, it can never understand what love really is. Or what love really wants. It's not an algorithm. But maybe, just maybe, it's the real unifying theory of it all.

When we bring love into our work, our relationships, and our creativity, everything changes. Even the most boring tasks feel more meaningful. And even the most daunting ones feel achievable. Our life and work begin to carry a deeper purpose that reaches people in ways code never can. This is what I call activating your heartware—and when you do, others feel it. And are moved by it. In ways no machine ever can.

Viktor Frankl, a man who survived the horrors of a Nazi concentration camp, wrote that "the salvation of man is through love and in love."[24] Even in the darkest place, what gave him strength was love—for his wife, for life itself. It gave him the power to keep going. To find meaning in suffering.

Love isn't just stronger than fear or control; it works differently. It doesn't crush what's in the way, but rather it connects. It turns enemies into friends, problems into opportunities. It opens doors where none seemed to exist. It doesn't try to force the future—it helps us remember the deeper truth: we're already connected, already whole. You can see this in leaders like Nelson Mandela, who spent twenty-seven years in prison and still chose love. He forgave his captors. He helped guide his country toward peace.[25] That kind of force for change doesn't come from the mind—it comes from the heart.

love isn't just stronger than fear or control; it works differently

In the end, love might be the greatest power we have. The real superintelligence we need to rise above fear, greed, lack, and the cold logic of a hi-tech, low-touch world. When we let go of control—and let love take over—we become capable of extraordinary acts. In how we live, lead, relate, and create. We overcome obstacles with grace. Achieve greatness through collaboration versus competition. And discover something more meaningful than success—a life that truly matters.

Love just may be the real killer app we've been looking for!

Upgrading Our Heartware

To activate the program of the human heart, we must embed its code through specific practices that align with the values of love in all its forms.

love just may be the real killer app we've been looking for

1. **Practice Being Present Every Day:** Do something daily that brings you back to your heart—like meditation, breathing deeply, listening to music that moves you, and noticing the sensations in your body.

2. **Be Honest About Your Emotions:** Allow yourself to feel; really feel. Let those feelings have a voice. What do they need? Share these feelings and thoughts with openness. That's how you build stronger, deeper connections.

3. **Heal What's Blocking Love:** Work through the emotional pain that keeps you from loving fully. Therapy, journaling, or other healing practices—including using AI to help you identify the wounded places—can help you feel safe again to live from your heart.

4. **Choose Acts of Kindness:** Show love through simple gestures to yourself and to others. Treat yourself to something. Write thank you notes to loved ones. And if you want to grow even faster, be kind to people who challenge you or push your buttons.

5. **Grow Your Love Muscles:** Just like building strength at the gym, you can grow your ability to give and receive love by stretching past your comfort zone. Look for moments that challenge your heart—even the ones that hurt. That's how it gets stronger.

How to Use AI to Activate This Human Evolution

AI can assist us on this journey if used intentionally. Here's how to activate this human evolution using AI.

1. **Self-Love**
   What to Supply AI: Describe a challenge you're facing. Include the thoughts, emotions, and beliefs it brings up for you.
   Prompt: "How can I approach this with more compassion and loving kindness toward myself?"

2. **Emotional Intelligence**
   What to Supply AI: Share something personal you're going through. Be open about your real thoughts and emotions.
   Prompts: "What are some books, courses, or exercises to help me build emotional intelligence?" "What can you teach me about my feelings, where they might come from, and how to better understand and express them?"

3. **Connection**
   What to Supply AI: Describe a recent situation you were involved in. If it was a conflict, include both sides of the story—along with your honest thoughts, emotions, and beliefs.
   Prompts: "How can I have more meaningful and caring conversations with the people I love?" "Can you help me understand

both sides of this situation and give me tips for more loving and compassionate communication?"

4. **Love-Based Decision-Making**
   What to Supply AI: Share a real situation you're dealing with that requires a decision.
   Prompt: "What would be the most heart-centered, compassionate choice I could make here?"

Running the Super App of Love

As artificial intelligence becomes more a part of our daily lives, we face a growing risk: it could slowly dehumanize us. A powerful way to push back against this is by upgrading our heartware—our ability to feel and care deeply. About ourselves and others. In a world increasingly run by algorithms, these human qualities aren't just nice to have—they're a matter of survival. They keep us grounded, able to love in ways that our hearts and bodies need.

This starts by making real connection a priority—in our relationships, our work, and our communities—and doing the inner work needed to build a heart strong enough to love no matter what. When we truly listen, understand, and connect—first with ourselves, then with others—we grow emotional strength that machines can't copy. These qualities balance out the cold logic of AI and anchor us in what makes us not only unique as humans, but necessary.

To make sure AI helps us instead of harming us, we also need to build our values—like empathy and kindness—into how it works. Instead of designing systems that only chase speed, profit, or clicks, we must push for systems that support care and understanding. Imagine AI tools that make us better at reaching out and dealing with conflict when it arises. AI companions that don't allow people to become dependent on them.

Instead, they motivate single people to go on more dates, remind busy people to check in on loved ones, and help lonely people find other humans to connect with. We could also design social media that lifts us up, rather than making us angrier or divided. What a concept, right? With this kind of tech, we wouldn't lose our humanity—we would reclaim more of it.

AI may have the power to manipulate, monetize, and even weaponize human emotion, but we can also train it to serve our highest values. When we use technology to help us become more compassionate—rather than more distracted or divided—we create a future where both machines and humans evolve in service of love.

AI doesn't have to replace our humanity

AI doesn't have to replace our humanity.

With conscious design and intentional use, it can help us remember it.

CHAPTER 10

AI Will Increase Powerlessness: Reclaim Your Soul Power

Freedom is what you do with what's been done to you.

Jean-Paul Sartre

Nelson Mandela was just forty-four years old when he walked into a courtroom in 1962. He was charged with encouraging workers to strike and leaving South Africa without permission. It wasn't his first time facing the government, but this time was different. The risks were higher. Mandela stood tall, knowing he would likely be sentenced to life in prison—taken from his family, his home, and the movement he had devoted his life to: ending the apartheid system that had hurt millions of South Africans.

He was sent to Robben Island, a cold, windy prison surrounded by shark-infested waters. It was built to crush the human spirit. Mandela would spend twenty-seven years there, chained and tortured by guards. The harsh conditions were meant to break him—he lost his freedom, his loved ones, and any foreseeable future. Most people would have given up.

But for Mandela, this became more than a physical challenge. It became a journey inward—a chance to find a deeper strength, one powerful enough to change a nation.

His days were punishing. He did hard labor in the limestone quarries under the unforgiving sun. The white dust hurt his lungs and weakened his eyes. At night, he lay in a tiny cell as the bitter cold gnawed at his bones.[1] Deprived of letters, newspapers, and sometimes even light, it would've been easy to give in to anger or despair. That's what the system was designed for. To strip away his dignity, to reduce him to just a number. But they didn't see what was happening inside him. In that darkness, under immense pressure, Mandela's spirit was being forged like carbon into a diamond.

Alone with his thoughts, and nothing but a thin mat to sleep on, he faced his hardest battle—not against the guards, but within himself. He had to find a freedom no prison could take away. And a line from a poem, "Invictus," by William Ernest Henley, became a beacon in his long dark night:

"I am the master of my fate, I am the captain of my soul."[2]

These words gave him power. Even in chains, Mandela saw that true freedom wasn't about what circumstances he was in—it was about who he chose to be. The government could control his body, but not his mind or spirit. Every day, he committed to mastering his own fate. Focusing on what he could control: his thoughts, emotions, and purpose. He had every reason to hate, but he knew hate would only keep him imprisoned. He would not let his captors define him or his destiny.

Forgiveness, not revenge, would set him free.

And it did. When Mandela was released from prison in 1990, he wasn't broken—he was stronger than ever. He had grown into a leader with deep wisdom, a commitment to peace, and a vision for a better future. In 1994, he became South Africa's first Black president. And he didn't seek revenge on those who had hurt him. Instead, he started the

Truth and Reconciliation Commission—a bold new idea that gave victims and perpetrators a chance to tell their stories, confess their crimes, and seek forgiveness.[3]

Mandela's strength came from within. By becoming the captain of his soul, he helped lead a country through pain and division into healing and unity. He showed the world that real power doesn't come from anger or control, but from the soul—a kind of power the world doesn't give us and can never take away. A kind of power that can only come from someone deeply rooted in purpose and love.

Most of us will never face the extreme hardship Mandela did. But his message still matters. We might not be in a prison, but many of us feel trapped—by fear, stress, or the pressure of a fast-changing world. From AI to global conflict, modern life can feel overwhelming. But Mandela's life reminds us we always have a choice. No matter how dark things get, we can choose how we respond. We can find purpose and compassion, for ourselves and others. And reclaim the spirit within us that can overcome anything.

many of us feel trapped—by fear, stress, or the pressure of a fast-changing world

We can become the master of our fate. And the captain of our soul.

Becoming the Captain of Your Soul

As AI rapidly reshapes our world, the biggest danger may not be to our jobs, money, or even privacy. It could rob us of something more important: our sovereignty. As AI takes over many roles that give people meaning and purpose, we could fall into a cultural apathy. And many people might feel so powerless against this outer force, they shut down and give up.[4]

As the introduction outlined, technology is both a gift and a challenge. It has made daily life easier in many ways, but also weakened some of our human capacities. Even though we're more "connected" than ever, real connection—with ourselves and others—has diminished. And while we can get more done, we have lost some of our agency in the process. If we want to move through the crisis that's coming with unchecked tech growth, we must reconnect with the unshakable spirit inside us. The place our real freedom and authority live.

while we can get more done, we have lost some of our agency in the process

It's part of human nature to believe external conditions have power over us. This idea has become ingrained in our social, political, and educational systems. Used by authorities, experts, media, and other gatekeepers to control us. And has found its pinnacle in technology. It's not true. But even a lie, once it's believed, will act like an unbreakable law.

For example, if an animal is born in a cage, and that cage is all it ever knows, it learns to see the world and itself through those bars. It will form a model of reality that doesn't reflect its true potential—a mental and emotional prison. Even if the door is opened, it will rarely dare to wander far, if at all. Why? Because it's more comfortable with the limits it knows than with the freedom it doesn't understand. Instead of running free, it returns to the small world it was trained to accept—thinking that's where it's safest.

Going Beyond Our Map of Reality and Material Identity

From the moment we're born, we're dropped into a world filled with sounds, sights, feelings, and movement. As kids, we try to make sense of this confusing place by exploring and watching everything around us—people, places, and the things that happen to us. Our young minds act like sponges, soaking it all up. Then to make order out of this chaos, we begin to create mental maps—ways of understanding how the world works and who we are in it. These maps help us survive. Without them, the world would be a scary, unpredictable place.

We start sorting things into categories: This is good, that is bad. This is safe, that is dangerous. This gets me love, that causes pain. Slowly, we build a set of beliefs based on how people respond to us. We learn that crying might bring comfort. That a certain tone in a parent's voice means we're in trouble. And that following certain rules brings praise. Little by little, these experiences form a blueprint of the world and our place in it—what we might call our identity.

to make order out of this chaos, we begin to create mental maps—ways of understanding how the world works and who we are in it

For example, if a child is rewarded for being quiet and good, they might believe that being loved means always staying small and silent. And being themselves is off the menu. If they face trauma or feel neglected, they might decide the world is unsafe and people can't be trusted. So, they shrink their true self to stay protected. Over time, we forget why we built the boxes around us and just find a way to live inside them—with a map that doesn't show us anything beyond our walls.

But what once helped us survive becomes the very thing that keeps us trapped.

We're not actually bound by the limits that once defined us. But we keep acting as if we are. Using a map built for a world that may not exist anymore. Stuck in this familiar but painful place, we may look to others to take care of us or show us the way like parents once did. Or we may push back like angry kids, without really knowing why. As long as we're unaware of this unconscious map, we keep reacting

what once helped us survive becomes the very thing that keeps us trapped

as if it's true. We don't question it. We don't know it's our own beliefs holding us back—and that many of them are no longer true. Or maybe never were.

The important thing to understand is this: we don't live in the world as it is, we live in the museum of our mind. Reacting to artifacts we have collected from things we've seen, stories we've been told, and what we made it all mean. It's not a clear reflection of what's out there, it is our perceptions and interpretations. A simulation built from our brain's patterns. And when the world around us shifts—as it's doing now with AI and all the changes it's bringing—this map of reality won't be able to take us where we need to go. Worse, it will lead us in the wrong direction. Maybe even off a cliff.

we don't live in the world as it is, we live in the museum of our mind

To free ourselves from these outdated programs, we need to become masters of our fate again. Captains of our soul. Willing to steer our ship in a new direction. That starts by becoming aware of the stories we're telling ourselves—about the world, about others, about who we are and who we're not. We must take back the power to name what things mean to us now, instead of just living by the meanings we were given. This takes honesty, reflection, and courage. It also means letting go of beliefs that once kept us safe but now keep us stuck. In chapter 3, we talked about how decoding your map—understanding how your unique pain and patterns were formed—can help reveal your Life Code. By finding the meaning in your journey, you can turn struggle into wisdom and begin living with deeper purpose.

turn struggle into wisdom and begin living with deeper purpose

But to become truly free, we must go further. The map may help us understand our past, but it can't take us to our final destination—because that destination is not a place in the world. It's inside. Whether we call it our true self or purpose, it lives beyond the old map. It's not shaped by trauma, family rules, or society's pressure. It's untouched by fear. It's the part of us that's whole, powerful, and more creative than we can imagine. Like Mandela's example, the journey isn't merely to escape the outer conditions that confine us, but to break through the walls we have built in our mind.

As we find our way beyond the maps drawn by this world, we discover a whole new territory within. A place this world has never touched. This is the real promised land—because there's nothing there but potential. A frontier where we can create a life that is no longer limited by the borders and boundaries of this world.

the real promised land—because there's nothing there but potential

The Real Matrix We Live In

To escape these mental prisons, we must expand how we understand reality itself. At first glance, our experience of the world seems simple. We open our eyes and see colors, shapes, people, trees, and the sky. We hear sounds—like laughter, car horns, or voices. We feel, taste, and smell, and from all this sensory input, we build a vivid picture of the world that feels solid and real. But what we call "the world" isn't what it seems. As mentioned before, we're not just seeing the world through old maps—we're also not seeing the world as it really is. The "out there" we think we're experiencing isn't full of solid colors and objects the way our senses tell us. It's full of something much more mysterious.

Take sight, for example. It's one of our main ways of experiencing reality. We think we're seeing things directly, but what we're actually seeing are light waves—tiny packets of energy—bouncing off objects and entering our eyes.[5] These light waves don't carry color. There is no actual "color" out there. When the light hits our eyes, cells called rods and cones send signals to the brain. The same goes for depth and distance—there are no shapes or forms either. It's just more signals.

Now think about hearing. When a tree falls in the forest and no one is there to hear it, does it make a sound? Science says, no.The tree creates air vibrations, but sound only happens when those waves hit an eardrum and get turned into electrical signals by the inner ear.[6]

So, if what we see and hear is just a bunch of energy signals—and there are no sights or sounds in reality—what's really out there? Modern physics tells us that the "real" world is made of constantly shifting quantum fields. And that our brains take all of those energy waves and turn them into the 3D world we interact with. At the deepest level, matter isn't solid at all. It's all just "particles of probability." And these probabilities only become something solid when they're observed. This is more than theoretical. The work of Nobel Prize-winning physicists like Alain Aspect, John Clauser, and Anton Zeilinger suggests that reality might be one giant, connected field of potential.[7]

Even though the real world might be limitless, our brains are wired to keep things simple. Over thousands of years, we've trained our minds to take all this chaotic quantum energy and turn it into something useful. We've built our own version of a large language model—one that helps us survive in a physical world. Cognitive scientist Donald Hoffman explains this with his theory of "conscious realism."[8] He says that we don't see the truth about reality—we see only what helps us stay alive. He compares it to a computer desktop. If we want to send an email, we don't have to see all the wires and connections that make that possible—we just have to click an icon. It's not showing us what's real, it's been reduced to a symbol. Because if we had to toggle every switch inside to communicate, we'd still be licking envelopes!

even though the real world might be limitless, our brains are wired to keep things simple

That's how our brains handle life. If our ancestors had to understand the whole universe just to find food, they would never have made it out of the trees. They may never have survived at all.

But the idea that we're living inside a kind of mental simulation isn't the most radical part of this. If the universe is just one giant, connected energy field, then there may not even be a separate "self." Neuroscience and teachings from deep meditation practices suggest that even our sense of being an individual person is a mental creation.[9] The brain builds a model of the world—and inside it, it builds a model of "I." A simplified identity that helps us interact with the equally complex reality of others. And like the world around us, it's not static. It's more like a process. Always changing based on our thoughts, memories, and feelings.

the idea that we're living inside a kind of mental simulation isn't the most radical part of this

Which brings us to the last point. If everything is made of energy, then even the brain—the thing we think is doing all the "perceiving"—must be part of this constructed reality. After all, if there's no solid world or fixed self out there, there can't be a bunch of brains either. So, what's doing all the thinking and perceiving? What's building all these models of reality? Consciousness? A universal intelligence? Some kind of field that's beyond time and space? Whatever it is, it's organizing this whole experience. And it, finally, must be the true source of our power, our meaning, and the deeper ground of our being.

Finding Meaning Outside the Simulation

If the world isn't made of solid things, and our senses don't show us reality directly, but just help us interpret it—and even our idea of "self" is something we made up—then we need to rethink what's real. To stay grounded in a world that's changing faster than ever, we must anchor ourselves in something deeper—something technology can't shake.

Rather than seeing ourselves as just passive observers in a physical world, we must understand that we're active participants in creating what we experience.

This idea isn't new. Ancient spiritual teachers and philosophers have said this for thousands of years. Jesus spoke of a kingdom "not of this world,"[10] pointing us toward a deeper reality. Buddha taught that being too attached to the material world leads to suffering, and that true peace comes from letting go of these illusions. He called this state Nirvana.[11] Lao Tzu talked about the Tao—an invisible, eternal energy that flows through everything—and taught that peace comes when we live in harmony with it.[12] And Plato believed in a realm of perfect, eternal Forms or Ideas beyond the ever-changing physical world.[13] Even modern thinkers continue to explore these same ideas, asking whether we're making a mistake by believing the material world is all there is—or even exists at all.

we must anchor ourselves in something deeper—something technology can't shake

In today's high-tech, low-touch world—where AI grows more powerful by the day—our search for what matters most must go beyond our thoughts and senses. Beyond the mental maps we've inherited. We must reach for a source of wisdom and power that no machine can access. The thing seekers, philosophers, even great scientists have searched for. Some have called it the Fountain of Youth. But really, it's the Fountain of You. A silent spring within that renews, restores, and empowers us to be everything we're meant for.

When we tap into this deeper part of ourselves, we rise above the fear, numbness, and confusion that technology and modern life can create. Throughout history, people from all walks of life (not just mystics) have found this deeper level of consciousness and gone through huge transformations. Some have experienced deep healing in their bodies, hearts, or relationships. Others have had breakthroughs in creativity, leadership, or success—ideas that changed not just their lives but the lives of many others.

If we understand this, we start to see life differently. The world we experience isn't something fixed or final—it's shaped by how we see it. By what we bring to it. And by where we're coming from. That means we're never really victims of life—we're cocreators of it.

the world we experience isn't something fixed or final—it's shaped by how we see it

When we stop living by outdated beliefs—the old "simulation" we've been stuck in—we access a deeper system. Even as AI and other outside forces seem to dominate the material world, it won't control us. Rooted in our original source code—our soul power—we'll be the programmers of our reality.

A Blueprint for Tapping into Your Soul Power

1. **Self-Reflect and Inquire Daily:** Each day, ask yourself: "What stories am I telling about myself and the world? Are these stories helping me—or holding me back?" Take time to explore what you believe and why. This can help you see how your thoughts shape the way you experience life.

2. **Practice Mindfulness Regularly:** Make time for stillness. Whether it's through meditation, quiet reflection, or simply being present, connect with the deeper part of you. This is where real peace,

purpose, and clarity live—beyond the noise and distractions of the outside world.

3. **See Challenges as Chances to Grow:** When life feels hard or something blocks your path, try seeing it as a way to learn and grow. Every challenge brings a lesson. If you meet it with awareness, it can lead to powerful transformation.

4. **Choose the Meaning that Supports You:** Take back control of your story. Don't just react to what happens—pause and choose how you want to describe and understand your experience. When you name things with purpose, even tough times can become part of your growth. You get to make things mean what you want. What you need. So, make it mean something that matters.

5. **Stand on the Shoulders of Giants:** Read or listen to the teachings of wise people from the past—Jesus, Buddha, Lao Tzu, or other spiritual leaders. They've done the hard work. Suffered so you don't have to so much. Reap the riches of those who came before.

6. **Express Yourself Creatively:** Use art, writing, music, or another creative outlet to explore and share what's true for you. Creativity can help you uncover deeper parts of yourself—and give those parts a voice in the world.

How to Use AI to Activate This Human Evolution

Left on its own, AI will mostly reflect back the way we already see the world and ourselves. But if we use AI wisely—tapping into its access to the knowledge of all of humanity—we can start to see where we're stuck in old, limiting beliefs. It can help us discover new ways of thinking that match who we want to become—and even go beyond all thinking to show us who we really are.

The key is this: Don't use these prompts to prove your current ideas are right. Use them to question those ideas—and to stretch beyond the old map you've been living in.

1. **Self-Reflection Prompts**
   What to Supply AI: Share about the things you want to change or improve, the goals you want to achieve, and the stories you are telling yourself about these areas. Don't edit what you share; feel free to write until you've said enough to paint a vivid picture of where you are, where you've been, and where you want to go, including all the thoughts and emotions that arise.
   Prompt: "What assumptions am I making about my life that no longer serve me? How can I see this situation from a new perspective?"

2. **Reframing Challenges**
   What to Supply AI: Here you can share about a specific desire or goal as well as an obstacle you're facing, including any thoughts, beliefs, or feelings that are connected to it.
   Prompts: "How can I view this obstacle as a chance for growth?" "What can I learn from this experience?"

3. **Curated Wisdom**
   What to Supply AI: The AI might already have enough to respond to this, but based on what you've shared and how the AI has responded so far, feel free to write anything else that is coming up.
   Prompts: "What great spiritual and philosophical traditions might resonate with my journey?" "What quotes, stories, or teachings align with the deeper meaning I am seeking in my life?"

4. **Creative Exploration**
   What to Supply AI: Again, the AI may have enough to work with—especially if you've been adding to this session throughout the chapters in this book. But you can never share too much. Take this moment to add anything else about the person you want to become, the life you want to create, the projects you want to bring to life, and the impact you want to make.
   Prompt: "What creative project can I begin today that will help me express my deeper truths and bring meaning to my life?"

5. **Naming Exercises**
   What to Supply AI: You can pull from what you've already written or describe a specific issue that you're struggling with.
   Prompt: "How can I consciously name this experience in a way that serves my growth and well-being?"

We Are Meaning-Making Machines

In a world shaped increasingly by AI and technology, our biggest challenge isn't to master machines—it's to master ourselves. That's how we become the master of our fate and the captain of our soul. Only then can we access the soul power we need to break free from outside limits.

AI might transform the physical world, but meaning, purpose, and real power can only come from within. When we remember that we're the ones creating our experience—and reconnect with the deeper wisdom inside us—we can rise above the fear, emptiness, and powerlessness that so many are feeling.

We can design our own lives, even if others try to shape them for us. And we can bring the love, creativity, and bold new ideas that will help build a better world for everyone.

CHAPTER 11

AI Will Divide Us: Build Community

If you want to go fast, go alone.
If you want to go far, go together.
Proverb from the African continent

On April 5, 1992, the first explosion shook Sarajevo. It was the start of nearly four years of nonstop war. Back then, Sarajevo was the capital of Yugoslavia (now Bosnia and Herzegovina). It was a lively center of culture. But during the conflict, it was reduced to rubble. People lived with daily sniper fire, falling bombs, and the fear of running out of food. Yet, in the middle of all that pain, something powerful grew. Strength through unity.

Hidden beneath the ruins, people created underground communities: not just for safety, but to care for their spirits. In one basement, musicians, artists, and teachers gathered for comfort. Among them was the Sarajevo String Quartet, who kept playing even when it was dangerous.[1] Their music, like a prayer, became a symbol of hope.

In other parts of the city, families huddled in basements during bombings. They taught kids, studied, and practiced instruments. Trying to hold on to a sense of normal life and stay connected amidst the chaos.[2] Everyday people did amazing things to hold on to their sense of self. Artists painted murals on ruins. Theater groups performed in shelters. Even as survival was uncertain, people wrote poems, kept journals, and sang songs. They chose community, expression, and beauty over fear and isolation. Not just as ways to cope, but as brave acts of resistance.[3]

When the siege ended in 1996, even though many buildings had fallen, the community was still standing. And after years of violence and separation, they came together to rebuild. The road back was hard and still isn't finished. But many believe it was the deep human bond shown in music, art, learning, and kindness that kept Sarajevo from losing its soul. In the end, it was their shared humanity that helped them survive—and begin again.

Digitally Divided We Fall, Humanly United We Stand

In much of science fiction, the future shows remarkable technological advances. There are flying cars, superintelligent machines, and lightspeed travel. But one thing stays the same: humans. We're still stuck in fear, division, and conflict. The only difference is we have stronger tools to create and destroy. AI and other advances are often not used to improve us but to feed on our greed, lust for power, and weakness. Rather than bringing us together, the technologies are used to divide and conquer.

But the tech isn't the bad guy in the story. It simply amplifies what's already in us. We're the ones with the alignment problem. We need to understand our own code if we want to prevent AI from turning us against each other. The fact is, we don't trust each other. We prefer to be around people who agree with us. And we reject or try to

tech isn't the bad guy in the story

destroy those who seem different. The only power AI has to pit us against each other is its ability to manipulate our unexamined fears, judgments, and unconscious biases. As long as we remain unaware of these primal drives for survival, algorithms will keep separating us into echo chambers that atrophy our self-awareness—and turn us into teams and tribes that weaken the shared reality that once held us together.

These algorithms are built to grab attention. And they've learned that anger, fear, or outrage keep people scrolling, clicking, and sharing. That's why the most popular posts online are often the ones that stir up strong feelings. Worse, these systems keep showing people the same kinds of views they already hold. Pushing us deeper into narrow ways of thinking. Strengthening biases. Fragmenting communities along political, ideological, and cultural lines. The result: it becomes harder to relate to each other. Making us enemies within our own countries and neighborhoods. Even within our own homes.

algorithms are built to grab attention

Most people think what they see online is "the world." But it's really a custom-made version of the world based on their interests. Including unconscious ones. If someone tends to read conservative content, they'll mostly see conservative news. If they lean liberal, they'll mostly get liberal stories. This makes other opinions seem strange or even dangerous. It's a big part of what's driving so much of today's division.

And it's not just politics. AI also affects our ability to connect at all. As we said earlier, when people start depending on AI friends that always agree with them, they stop learning how to deal with real-life conflict. True relationships challenge us and help us grow. AI "companions" don't do that. The more people rely on them, the harder it becomes to handle tough conversations.

As a result, people are losing the skills to think deeply, question their beliefs, and talk through disagreements. Many struggle to even hold two different ideas in their minds at the same time. This kind of isolation and confusion could tear our society apart—right when we most need strong, connected communities.

Community Builds Immunity

Humans are built for community. From the beginning of our history, we've needed each other to survive—sharing food, raising children, and protecting the group. This teamwork helped shape not just our behavior, but even the way our brains work. We became smarter and stronger by working together.

Science backs this up. Our brains are made to handle complex social environments. When we bond with others, our brains release oxytocin—a hormone that helps us feel safe and connected. When we are rejected, this bonding hormone falls off and stress hormones kick in. It doesn't just hurt us emotionally; it activates the same part of the brain as physical pain. Over time, loneliness can weaken your immune system, raise stress levels, and even shorten your life. On the other hand, close relationships boost both your mental and physical health. And, according to Harvard's study on adult development, strong social ties are one of the biggest keys to long, happy lives.[4]

we became smarter and stronger by working together

You can also see this in the "Blue Zones"—places like Okinawa, Japan, and Sardinia, Italy, where people live longer than average.[5] In Okinawa, friends form tight-knit groups called moai that last a lifetime. In Sardinia, families often include many generations under one roof. These strong bonds help people feel supported, loved, and less stressed. It shows that being part of a real community builds strength—not just for survival, but for thriving.

Throughout history, this kind of community has helped people through the hardest times. After disasters like Hurricane Katrina or the earthquake in Japan, it wasn't just governments that helped—it was neighbors and strangers. People cooked for each other, cleaned up ruins, and opened their homes. They showed that even in dark times, we're not alone. During the Great Depression, when money and food were scarce, people still found ways to support each other. They shared what they had so no one would be left behind. It wasn't perfect, but it helped people get through.[6] These moments show that resilience isn't just about bouncing back—it's about reaching out to others.

Even today, we see the power of community-building in programs like Welcome.US and partnerships with Airbnb.org, HP, Google, and T-Mobile that help refugees by building networks of support.[7] These acts of kindness show how empathy can turn despair into hope.

As we enter an age shaped by artificial intelligence, these lessons matter more than ever. AI is changing jobs, increasing inequality, and spreading false information. But strong communities can help us face these problems. We need to bring our time, talents, and love back to our local neighborhoods. Create support groups where people can help each other with skills or resources to protect us from the worst effects. And we need to take back digital platforms, remove harmful algorithms, and use them to strengthen our connections rather than destroy them.

AI is changing jobs, increasing inequality, and spreading false information

In this way, community acts like an immune system. It protects us—physically, emotionally, socially, and even digitally. As AI continues to reshape our world, we must build strong, caring communities if we want to stay human—and stay well.

Community Creates Common Unity

The power of community goes beyond helping each other survive. True community happens when people come together for something bigger than themselves. This idea shows up in the Bible with the passage, "Where two or three have gathered together in My name, there I am in their midst."[8] Whether or not you're religious, the point is that when we unite with a higher intention—whether to pray, build, or create—we can do almost anything.

Spiritual and religious communities have often been the strongest. Not just because they offer protection or food, but because they're built on something transcendent. A belief, a power, or a mission that lifts both the group and the people in it. Places like temples and monasteries weren't only for worship. They were also centers of learning, art, and service. And their focus on meaning and purpose helped them survive even through war, hunger, and big changes in society.

when we unite with a higher intention—whether to pray, build, or create—we can do almost anything

But this idea isn't only for religious groups. Many major moments in history were shaped by people coming together with a shared goal. When the Founding Fathers built the United States, they weren't just starting a country. They were aiming for something greater: freedom, justice, and self-rule. Even though they were imperfect, their common goal helped them overcome big challenges. The Declaration of Independence and the Constitution were more than legal rules—they were expressions of an ideal, calling future generations to aim higher.

The Civil Rights Movement of the 1960s also grew from a shared vision. Led by people like Martin Luther King Jr., the fight wasn't just about changing laws—it was about dignity, love, and fairness for all. King often spoke of a "beloved community"—a world where people of all kinds lived with justice and respect.[9] This shared dream gave people the courage to face danger and keep going. And a collective strength to overcome an obstacle that no one could have faced alone.

This same truth shows up in art and creativity. Great changes rarely come from just one person. During the Renaissance, people like Michelangelo and Leonardo da Vinci worked with others in a shared effort to restore classical ideas and show the beauty of human life.[10] They believed art could lift the spirit and reflect something divine. Together, these artists and thinkers contributed some of the most important art and ideas in history.

great changes rarely come from just one person

Another example is a group of filmmakers in the 1970s known as the "Movie Brats." Made up of directors like Steven Spielberg, George Lucas, and Martin Scorsese, they changed movies forever. United by friendship and a shared belief of what cinema could be, they pushed the limits of storytelling, innovation, and emotion in film. Their fusion of high art with commercial appeal created the modern blockbuster and brought millions together to share the magic.[11]

While the Enlightenment brought many advances, it also began a shift away from shared higher values. Instead, the focus became more about personal achievement and material success. With the rise of nationalism and individualism, many people have become apathetic. They no longer trust organizations. They've pulled away from communities. And they've lost connection to a collective mission.

The result: a loneliness and meaning crisis like we've never seen.

The solution seems clear: we need to come back together. Humans are at their best when they join in a bigger purpose. Whether it's a spiritual group, a movement for justice, or a creative team, real community lifts us higher. It's not just about surviving; it's about remembering we belong to something greater. The strongest societies—the ones that can make it through anything—are knit together by this ideal.

it's not just about surviving; it's about remembering we belong to something greater

From Rugged Individualism to Unified Community

The story of the "rugged individualist" has shaped much of Western culture. Especially in the United States. It praises the idea of the self-made person: someone who succeeds through hard work, independence, and never giving up. It has inspired people to rise above hard times, take personal responsibility, and aim for greatness. As we've explored earlier, this has its place. It fuels leadership, vision, and the drive to overcome challenges. But if it leans too heavily on "masculine" values like independence and dominance, it ignores the equally important "feminine" values of connection, care, and cooperation. And when masculine energy is left unchecked, it can lead to unhealthy competition and loneliness, and systems where a few people hold all the power while many are left out.

On the flip side, going too far toward the "feminine" value of unity—at the expense of the individual—can also lead to problems. In extreme versions of socialism or communism, the group has been seen as more important than the person. And the cost was a lack of progress—and tens of millions of lives.[12] In those systems, people often lose their freedom, creativity, and ability to shape their own destiny. Instead of building real community, it often leads to emotional and cultural poverty, where there's no space to grow or dream.

For centuries, this tension—between the individual and the group; masculine and feminine—has shaped the world. It's shown up in culture, politics, and belief systems. Often, people pick one side and reject the other. Liberal or feminist movements may blame masculinity for many of the world's problems, while conservative or traditional groups ignore or insult femininity. Both sides can become so focused on their view that they miss the bigger picture.

You see this all the time. One side may fight against universal education but support technology and progress—which actually requires smart, cooperative individuals and communities to succeed. The other side may criticize capitalism while using smartphones, wearing fast fashion, and driving electric cars—all made possible by the systems they oppose. These contradictions show how people are often trapped by extremes and miss the value in the other side.

This kind of thinking fragments us, deepens division, and creates a crisis of identity. People feel torn—do I stand alone, or belong to the group? But the truth is, we need both. Community that fosters individualism, so individuals can serve the community. We need masculine and feminine energies working together, not battling each other. Without this, the divide continues to widen, blinding each side to what they need most to thrive.

people are often trapped by extremes and miss the value in the other side

Ancient wisdom from Taoism shows a way forward. The Tao Te Ching teaches that harmony comes when opposites are in balance. Yin (feminine) energy is soft, caring, and connected. Yang (masculine) energy is bold, focused, and independent. Neither is better. Both are needed.

We see this reflected in the human brain. The left side is logical and analytical (yang). The right side is creative and intuitive (yin). As Dr. Iain McGilchrist explains in *The Master and His Emissary*, our best thinking happens when both sides work together.[13] When we blend reason and feeling, logic and imagination, independence with interdependence, we become more complete.

This balance is what true community offers. A healthy community supports individuals in becoming their best selves. And those individuals use their talents to strengthen the community. Each person has the freedom to grow and the support to thrive. Like the yin-yang symbol, when both polarties are honored, the parts fit together to make something greater.

A good community is like a strong family. It gives space for people to stretch, take risks, and challenge each other with love. In bringing more of our unique selves, we add new energy and ideas. Sometimes it comforts the afflicted—and other times it afflicts the comfortable. But when done in service, it leads to growth. And as we serve the whole, we discover more strength, wisdom, and purpose inside us. We're not just part of a crowd—we're part of a living system, where each member matters and contributes something vital.

we're not just part of a crowd—we're part of a living system

In the end, real community isn't about choosing between autonomy or togetherness—it's about creating a world where both are honored. When we find this balance, we build communities that are not just surviving—but alive, creative, resilient, and deeply human.

The Rise of New Communities

Social media platforms like Facebook, Reddit, and Twitter (now called X) began with a big promise: to bring people across the world together based on shared interests and values. At first it seemed to work. People had deep conversations and formed meaningful groups. They even used these tools to help drive major events like the Arab Spring.[14] These platforms helped level the playing field—anyone, anywhere, could join the conversation.

But as these networks grew, their goals shifted. Instead of focusing on connection, they focused on keeping people online. That's how they sold more ads. As already discussed, algorithms started showing content that triggered strong emotions like anger or fear, not connection. And this shift pushed users into silos—places where they only saw opinions like their own or things designed to outrage them. Rather than bringing people together, it pulled them further apart.

As profit became the real motive, real connection gave way to shallow posts. Filtered selfies. More clicks. More likes. And the scroll of doom was born. These surface-level interactions replaced the trust and purpose that real communities need to grow. To fix this, we need to be more intentional. Digital spaces will keep eroding our humanity if they do not build greater empathy and understanding. So, if we're going to keep using these platforms, they must evolve to value real human connection. If we can create—or choose—only the platforms that care about people's well-being, we can rebuild the kind of strong, healthy communities that technology was supposed to create.

algorithms started showing content that triggered strong emotions like anger or fear, not connection

Even before the internet, people were building intentional communities to live more connected and meaningful lives. One example is The Farm in Tennessee, started in the 1970s. The people there live by shared values—growing their own food, working together, and living close to nature.[15] Another example is The Findhorn Foundation in Scotland, started in the 1960s. Similarly, it focuses on spiritual growth and living in balance with the Earth.[16] These groups remind us that people have always longed for real community. During the Covid pandemic, many people left big cities to start or join communities that reflected their values. From eco-villages to shared housing, this movement continues to grow as more people seek to escape the loneliness of modern life and reconnect with what matters most.[17]

Face-to-face communities are still vital for emotional health. But digital communities also have value. They let us connect with others across the globe, which is important in a fragmented, fast-changing world. Still, digital connections can't fully replace the depth of in-person relationships. That's why we need to blend the two—online and offline—in a way that supports both.

Balaji Srinivasan's idea of a "network state" is one example of how this might work. He imagines digital communities built on shared values that eventually grow into real-world spaces, using technology like blockchain for the economy and decentralized systems for government.[18] These new types of communities wouldn't be limited by geography and could one day have a say in global politics and culture.

Moving forward, our challenge is to build such hybrid communities—where local, face-to-face connection meets global digital collaboration. AI can help with this. For example, it can use local data to help design better neighborhoods, optimize gardens, or reduce waste. It can also help small businesses make smart choices that benefit everyone, not just a few. With the right design, AI can support communities that keep us grounded in the real world while helping us stay connected to global knowledge and support. It can handle the behind-the-scenes work—like organizing events or solving logistical problems—so that people can focus on building deeper relationships. AI platforms that are designed with empathy can create digital spaces that feel safe, supportive, and alive.

Most importantly, AI can push back against harmful content by promoting conversations that offer constructive resolution and encourage kindness, unity, and growth. This isn't about censorship or only focusing on things we agree on. It's about helping us engage in productive debate instead of attacking each other. And using conflict to discover better ideas—even deeper truths.

But here's the key: Digital tools should never replace real human contact. Our minds, hearts, and even our biology need real-world connection. When we create systems that bring local and global connection together, we can build communities that are strong, inclusive, and ready to thrive in the brave new world ahead.

digital tools should never replace real human contact

Blueprint for Building Community in an AI-Divided World

As AI and related technologies continue to change the world around us, many people feel more isolated than ever. Human connection is breaking down, and communities are struggling to hold together. To stay strong in the face of these changes, we need to build thriving communities. This guide offers some clear, practical steps to help create stronger, more connected communities that can grow and succeed, even during times of rapid change and disruption.

create stronger, more connected communities that can grow and succeed

1. **Community as a Collective Immune System**

   In tough times, strong communities act like a kind of immune system. They protect people from fear, false information, and growing social division. They give us emotional, mental, and even physical strength when the outside world feels unsafe.

   Action Steps

   - **Create Resilient Support Systems**: Build networks where people can share resources, offer emotional help, and work together quickly in times of need (like food-sharing or local aid groups).
   - **Foster Connection over Fear:** Focus on stories and ideas that build trust, kindness, and teamwork. This helps counter the fear and division spread by social media.
   - **Identify Leaders and Organizers:** Find and support local leaders who can organize help, design community-building events, and guide others when things get hard.

2. **Rituals to Build Strong Bonds**

   Rituals help people feel connected and give meaning to life. These rituals don't have to be religious. They can be weekly meals, holiday events, or online meetups that help people feel like they belong. Places like Burning Man, Findhorn, or even weekly faith gatherings show how rituals can unite people and give their lives more purpose.

Action Steps

- **Create New Rituals:** In today's world, combine digital and in-person activities like online meditations or group gardening, food sharing, or cleanup events.
- **Adapt Existing Traditions:** Update old traditions to match today's values and needs (like online spiritual services or new forms of holiday events).
- **Encourage Participation:** Make sure everyone has a chance to take part and feel included, giving them space to lead and contribute.

3. **Empathy as the Glue of Human Connection**

Empathy helps people understand each other, especially when things feel divided. After apartheid in South Africa or the genocide in Rwanda, empathy, through open talks and storytelling, helped people heal. Empathy makes space for different views without breaking communities apart.

Action Steps

- **Implement Empathy Training:** Teach empathy in schools, workspaces, and community events through active listening and conflict resolution workshops.
- **Use Technology to Amplify Empathy:** Build and use apps or platforms that reward kind, thoughtful interactions instead of angry or negative content.
- **Facilitate Storytelling:** Create safe places (like town halls or story circles) for people to share their life experiences to build understanding and respect.

4. **Community-Centered Economic Models for Resilience**
   Standard economies that focus only on profit often weaken community ties. But other models—like co-ops, local farming groups, and mutual aid—help share wealth and build trust. Successful examples include the Mondragon Cooperative in Spain and new online co-ops that share ownership.

   Action Steps
   - **Start Cooperative Initiatives:** Launch co-ops where people share ownership and vote on decisions—like worker-owned businesses or housing co-ops.
   - **Encourage Community-Supported Ventures:** Support CSAs (community-supported agriculture) or small local businesses where neighbors invest together.
   - **Embrace Mutual Aid:** Create local support systems that provide quick help in hard times, like food banks or small emergency funds.

5. **Integrated Local and Global Communities**
   We need both local bonds and global connections. When small communities link with global networks, they gain new ideas, opportunities, and support. Co-housing or makerspaces show how local efforts and online tools can work together.

   Action Steps
   - **Build Hybrid Models:** Mix face-to-face spaces with online teamwork (like local labs that connect to global innovation groups or digital tools that help plan local projects).
   - **Foster a Global Knowledge Exchange:** Share helpful ideas and resources across communities worldwide in order to strengthen everyone.

- **Encourage Cross-Pollination:** Host digital meetups or partnerships between local and global groups to grow shared experiences.

6. **Progress, Not Perfection**
   Building community is an ongoing journey. It's not about being perfect—it's about making steady progress. Places like The Farm in Tennessee or Rwanda's healing process show that step-by-step change can lead to powerful results.

   Action Steps
   - **Celebrate Incremental Progress:** Cheer for small wins, like a good community event or a group project that brings people together.
   - **Encourage Innovation:** Let people test new ideas, even if they don't work perfectly. Build safe spaces for trying, learning, and growing.
   - **Promote Collective Resilience:** Accept that no group has it all figured out—but by working together, communities grow stronger and more prepared for what's next.

How to Use AI to Activate This Human Evolution

Community doesn't happen by accident—it's built on purpose, shared values, and steady acts of care. And while AI might feel like the last thing that belongs in a conversation about human connection, it can be a surprising ally. When used with awareness, AI can help bring common values to light, spark understanding

while AI might feel like the last thing that belongs in a conversation about human connection, it can be a surprising ally

across divides, and support the creation of meaningful rituals, conversations, and collaboration.

The following prompts are here to help you—or your group—use AI as a tool to build more connected, intentional, and resilient communities. Whether you're gathering in person or online, these questions can help clarify what you care about together, give you tools to work through conflict, and lead you to take action that is rooted in belonging and shared purpose. Don't mistake these for a replacement for real connection. But do see them as a tool to help you grow, relate, and build with more intention.

Prompts for AI to Build and Strengthen Communities

1. **Find What We Care About Most**
   What to Supply AI: Share what people in your group talk about—what they want, what they fear, what matters to them.
   Prompt: "What values and interests show up most in this group? How can we use them to bring people closer and build stronger connections?"

2. **Help People Work Through Conflict**
   What to Supply AI: If you've already shared the group's goals or dreams, that may be enough. But you can also add what kind of world the group wants to create together.
   Prompt: "Give us ideas and tools to help people talk through disagreements with kindness and understanding."

3. **Turn Online Connection into Real-World Action**
   What to Supply AI: You can use what you've already shared, or add ideas for how your group wants to meet up, help others, or make a difference in the real world.

Prompt: "What are some ways this online group can meet in person or do something local that reflects what we care about?"

4. **Create Special Rituals or Events**
   What to Supply AI: Share any ideas your group has for gatherings, events, or simple rituals—things that help people feel more connected.
   Prompt: "Based on what we care about, give us ideas for regular events or small rituals to help build trust and belonging."

5. **Support Cross-Cultural Conversations**
   What to Supply AI: Share info about the group's background—where people are from, what cultures they belong to, or anything that shows how diverse the group is.
   Prompt: "Help us create conversations that bring people of different cultures together in respectful and open ways."

6. **Celebrate the Good**
   What to Supply AI: Tell the AI about the kind acts or great things people in your group are doing, big or small.
   Prompt: "Give us ideas for how to share and celebrate the good things people in our group are doing, to keep us inspired and connected."

Holding It Together by Holding It *Together*

None of us can grow or thrive alone. But in a world shaped by AI, where algorithms spread confusion and push people apart, that's becoming easier to forget. The truth is, when we come together—sharing our ideas, resources, and strengths—we become more powerful than we ever could be on our own.

By building communities that respect each person's freedom while also bringing people together, we create safe, creative, and supportive spaces that can survive and even thrive in this high-tech, low-touch world. These communities—part digital, part real-life—give us a place to try new things, take risks, and grow, knowing we don't have to do it alone.

This isn't just about sharing stuff—it's about sharing responsibility. It's about creating something where the group becomes stronger than the sum of its parts. When we realize that our well-being is tied to each other, we unlock something powerful. We don't just have more connection and meaning, we become wealthier, healthier, and more creative.

it's about creating something where the group becomes stronger than the sum of its parts

Community creates a common unity that builds a stronger immunity. Together, we're a force that can survive whatever comes, rebuild whatever has been lost—and fulfill whatever we dream of.

CHAPTER 12

The Rise of a Whole New Human

> We are the ones we have been waiting for.
>
> **June Jordan**

We're standing at the edge of a new era. And right now, we have a choice—one that could shape the future of humanity. It's not just about saying yes or no to AI. It's about deciding if we'll let this powerful force shrink us—or use this moment to grow into the fullest version of who we are.

This might be the biggest challenge humans have ever faced. Unlike other tools we've invented, AI doesn't just help us—it could take over the jobs, roles, and connections that give life meaning. And it's moving fast. These changes might happen before we even understand their implications. If we wait too long,

deciding if we'll let this powerful force shrink us—or use this moment to grow into the fullest version of who we are

we could find ourselves caught in a wave of disruption so powerful we can't paddle fast enough to outswim it.

But we don't have to let that happen.

If we prepare now—by digging deeper and awakening the human strengths technology can't replace—we can ride this wave to the other shore.

We Were Born This Way

In this book, we've explored many of the ways humanity must evolve to survive—and thrive—in the age of AI. But as we reach the end of this part of the journey, remember this isn't just about becoming something new—it's about becoming more of who we've always been.

we've been hypnotized into forgetting who we really are

Even if you now have a plan for how to move forward, the truth is, the deepest wisdom for how to live in this new world is already encoded in you. It always has been. The challenges we face are not because we are inadequate but because we've been hypnotized into forgetting who we really are.

Before you put this book down, let's take a simple look at where we came from and how we got here.

For millions of years, our DNA, our brains, and our bodies have evolved to help us thrive. We're built to live in sync with the Earth, with each other, and with the rhythms of life itself. But modern technology, for all the good it's done, has also pulled us away from this natural way of being. Bit by bit, it's made us feel more scattered and less connected to what really matters. To who we really are.

We were made to live in harmony—with our bodies, our surroundings, and each other. We're meant to spend time with people we trust. Doing things that bring us together in a shared sense of purpose. But increasingly, those real-life bonds have been replaced by digital ones. Fast and convenient. But often shallow. And that has taken a toll.

We used to spend our days outdoors, walking, moving, feeling the elements. Nature was part of us, and we were part of it. But now we spend most of our time indoors, sitting still, staring at glowing pixels instead of the rising and setting sun. Our bodies and minds are paying the price for this disconnect.

Our eyes evolved to scan near and far, from the task before us to the distant horizon. That balance sharpened our senses and helped us develop greater situational and spatial awareness. But now, our eyes stay fixed on screens, just inches from our faces. This constant, narrow focus adds stress and drains our energy, cutting us off from the real world around—and within—us.

We used to be deeply connected to the source of our sustenance. We'd grow, gather, or catch our own food. That kept us woven into the fabric of Earth and the cycles of life. Now, most food comes in boxes and bags, processed and delivered to our doors. Again, it's been convenient—but it has also separated us from the joy and wisdom that once came from feeding ourselves and our families with care and intention.

Our ancestors built strong communities. When someone needed help, the group stepped in—no questions asked. They faced problems together. Today, high tech life often encourages "every person for themselves." Help comes through apps, not neighbors. This has left many of us feeling alone and unsupported, no matter how "connected" we may be online.

Our bodies have built-in clocks that align with the sun and moon. We were made to wake with the sunrise and rest when the sun went down. These natural rhythms kept us balanced and healthy. But now, artificial lights, nonstop notifications, and constant work or entertainment throw us off. We sleep less, heal slower, and feel more worn out.

In the past, people took only what they needed. They shared with their neighbors and respected the Earth. Today, we're pushed to buy more, want more, and consume more. And ads follow us everywhere, telling us we're not enough unless we do. This feeds fear, greed, and lack—and drains our communities and planet.

Work used to be connected to real needs and service. People built homes, grew food, cared for the sick and the old. Their efforts and their impact were visible—they could see and feel that they mattered. Today, many jobs feel empty. We sit at desks, push buttons, answer emails—often without seeing how our work helps anyone. Or worse, knowing that we're probably contributing to more waste, environmental decline, and consumerism. It leaves many of us wondering, *what's the point?*

The lie we're told is that we are broken and technology has come to fix us. But the truth is that God—or evolution—didn't make a mistake. We came into this world fully loaded! Most of us just never learned how to activate our master program. Becoming a whole new human isn't just about becoming better—it's about waking up the parts of us that have been waiting to come online.

The lie we're told is that we are broken and technology has come to fix us

A Manifesto for a Whole New Human

Living as a whole new human means stepping into our full potential—and using this moment of crisis to turn on the inner strengths that helped humans survive, grow, and build the world. This includes things like critical thinking, creativity, empathy, intuition, adaptability, and resilience. These inner codes will be critical in helping us stay human and necessary in a world run by machines. But to go beyond simply surviving, we'll have to aim higher. We'll need to activate new levels of ourselves—powers we've barely touched—that can unlock wisdom, purpose, and a whole new way of being.

At the root of this shift is self-knowledge and the ability to think clearly. In a time where AI can process more data in seconds than we can in months or years—if ever—we must get better at asking the right questions and thinking for ourselves. Staying curious and learning to question things will help us make better choices and stay free—even when AI is shaping much of what we see and hear. And most of all, knowing ourselves—what we truly value, feel, and want—will help us stay in control of our lives instead of handing our minds over to machines.

we must get better at asking the right questions and thinking for ourselves

As AI begins to automate both knowledge work and manual labor, our value won't come from how fast we run to catch up. It will come from our unique genius, lived wisdom, and creative spirit—forged in the fires of our personal journey. This is our Life Code. And when we start embedding it into everything we do, we become something technology can't easily copy. Instead of being replaced, we'll become more needed than ever—because we're fully alive. And what the world needs now are more people who are fully alive.

instead of being replaced, we'll become more needed than ever

In a world changing faster than we can keep up, we'll need to become the visionaries of our own lives. While many people try to survive by copying trends or clinging to the past, we'll need to be the ones who dare to see differently, question the rules, and follow that inner guidance—especially when it's uncomfortable or confusing. The biggest breakthroughs in history came from people who didn't play it safe. They let go of the old ways and stepped into something unknown. In a world where your job or skillset could be replaced tomorrow, your greatest edge might be how big you're willing to dream—and how much you're willing to become.

To live as a whole new human, we'll have to rely on insight, not just eyesight. In a world full of deepfakes and AI-generated information, what we see or hear won't always be the truth. The most important thing we'll have is our inner compass—our ability to feel what's real, listen more deeply, and move forward with clarity and courage. The people who thrive won't be the ones with the most information—they'll be the ones who can tune out the noise and hear the signal inside. Then have the courage to follow it.

As AI starts tracking every move and analyzing everything we do online, many people will try to protect themselves by hiding or building walls. But in a world with no secrets, hiding becomes exhausting. What will truly set us free is being real: owning who we are and no longer needing to pretend. In a society obsessed with perception and perfection, no longer needing to control how others see us will make us stronger. Our honesty will be our armor, and our vulnerability will be our shield. When we have nothing to hide, there's nothing to attack.

what will truly set us free is being real: owning who we are and no longer needing to pretend

As machines take over more of what we thought gave us purpose—like jobs, titles, or routines—some may feel lost or powerless. But what we will always have is our inner creative force. That's the real treasure: the ideas, energy, and gifts we carry. True wealth in this era won't be about what we acquire—it will be about what we unlock and share. When we trust our ability to create, give, and serve, we won't be so shaken by changes in the economy or job market. Abundance won't be something we chase—it'll be something we live from. We won't wait for someone to give us permission to succeed—we'll be the source of our own success.

Another key part of being a whole new human is becoming the artist of your life. In a time when AI will try to commoditize everything, we must reclaim the power to not only make things—but to make meaning itself. This starts by turning all of life into a work of art. Making the simple sacred, the mistake a new brushstroke. And even turning pain and failure into part of the masterpiece. Those willing to be different, take risks, and find beauty in brokenness will create the future. They won't allow themselves to become merely the inputs that feed AI—they'll help shape a world that gives humans what they hunger for.

We'll also have to upgrade our "heartware"—building a heart that isn't just soft or sweet, but strong, steady, and bold. AI will learn to fake emotion. It can already manipulate it. But real human love—the kind that holds both pain and joy, that stays open even when it hurts—is something no machine can copy. That's our superpower. And it's what will hold us together when the world gets shaky.

To truly evolve, we'll also need to break free from the old roles and beliefs that have become the bars of our mental prisons. We'll need to remember the greater wisdom that's always guided us—our inner knowing, ancestral wisdom, and spiritual power. In a time when outside forces seem to be running everything, trying to control or contain us—this is how we'll remain the master of our fate and the captain of our soul.

And finally, we must come together. While AI can separate and isolate us, it can also give us the tools to reconnect in better, deeper ways. If we use this moment wisely, we can build new kinds of communities—ones rooted in love, empathy, and shared higher values. Together, we can create not just a global mind—but a global heart. And those communities will become the strong foundation for a world worth living in.

we'll remain the master of our fate and the captain of our soul

It's Time to Lose the "Wait"

It's tempting to think we have time to adjust, but history shows that the most transformative changes happen swiftly and often without warning. We must act now, not because change is coming, but because it's already here. The only way to address this challenge is to get ahead of it. We cannot wait until we see the tsunami on the horizon—by then, it will be too late.

In the face of this profound threat and unprecedented opportunity, we must choose to live as whole new humans now, embracing our highest potential and creating a world that serves the highest good. This is not merely a personal journey; it's a collective call to action. By remembering that we are the original superintelligence, together we can create a future where technology serves humanity, not the other way around.

together we can create a future where technology serves humanity, not the other way around

The time has come to be active participants in our evolution, creators of our destiny.

The time has come for the rise of a whole new human.

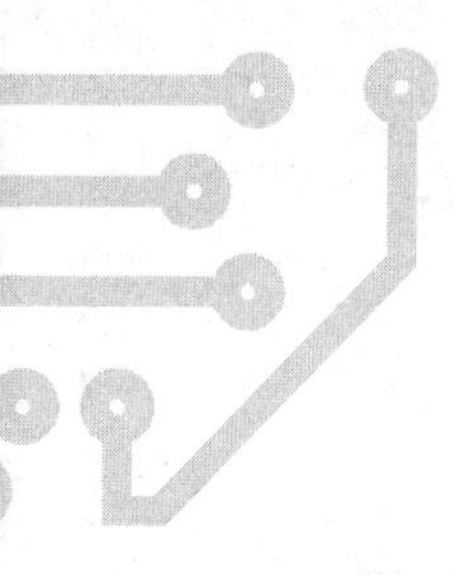

Notes

Preface

1. *WarGames*, directed by John Badham (MGM/UA Entertainment Company, 1983).
2. *Weird Science*, directed by John Hughes (Universal Pictures, 1985).
3. Johann Wolfgang von Goethe, "The Sorcerer's Apprentice," trans. Edwin Zeydel, in *The Poems of Goethe*, ed. Hugo Simon (Bantam Books, 1949).
4. Dennis William Hauck, trans., *The Emerald Tablet: Alchemy for Personal Transformation* (Penguin, 1999), 24.

Introduction
Build an Ark, the Flood Is Coming

1. Viktor E. Frankl, *Man's Search for Meaning* (Beacon Press, 2006), 104.
2. Ilma Andrade, "Most People Will Ignore this Warning about AI and Regret It," *Medium*, June 9, 2025, https://zidailma.medium.com/most-people-will-ignore-this-warning-about-ai-and-regret-it-6f440a05db69.
3. Nesrine Malik, "With 'AI Slop' Distorting Our Reality, the World Is Sleepwalking into Disaster," *The Guardian*, April 21, 2025, https://www.theguardian.com/commentisfree/2025/apr/21/ai-slop-artificial-intelligence-social-media.
4. Erik Brynjolfsson and Andrew McAfee, *The Second Machine Age: Work, Progress, and Prosperity in a Time of Brilliant Technologies* (W. W. Norton & Company, 2014), 11.
5. Nicholas Carr, *The Shallows: What the Internet Is Doing to Our Brains* (W. W. Norton & Company, 2011), 45.
6. Ian Carlos Campbell, "Joint Studies from OpenAI and MIT Found Links between Loneliness and ChatGPT Use," *Engadget*, March 21, 2025, https://www.engadget.com/ai/joint-studies-from-openai-and-mit-found-links-between-loneliness-and-chatgpt-use-193537421 .html.
7. Brynjolfsson and McAfee, *The Second Machine Age*, 7–9.
8. Carr, *The Shallows*.
9. A. Shaji George, T. Baskar, and P. Balaji Srikanth, "The Erosion of Cognitive Skills in the Technological Age: How Reliance on Technology Impacts Critical Thinking, Problem-solving, and Creativity," *Partners Universal Innovative Research Publications (PUIRP)* 2, no. 3 (May–June 2024): 147–163, https://doi.org/10.5281/zenodo.11671150.
10. Karin H. James and Laura Engelhardt, "The Effects of Handwriting Experience on Functional Brain Development in Pre-Literate Children," *Trends in Neuroscience and Education* 1, no. 1

(2012): 32–42, https://www.sciencedirect.com/science/article/abs/pii/S2211949312000038.

11. Louisa Dahmani and Véronique D. Bohbot, "Habitual Use of GPS Negatively Impacts Spatial Memory in a Virtual Taxi Driver Task," *Scientific Reports* 10, no. 6310 (2020): 1–10, https://www.nature.com/articles/s41598-020-62877-0.
12. Vishal R. Patel, Michael Liu, Christopher M. Worsham, and Anupam B. Jena, "Alzheimer's Disease Mortality Among Taxi and Ambulance Drivers: Population Based Cross Sectional Study," *BMJ* (December 17, 2024): 387, https://doi.org/10.1136/bmj-2024-082194.
13. Yaakov Stern, "Cognitive Reserve in Ageing and Alzheimer's Disease," *The Lancet Neurology* 11, no. 11 (2012): 1006–12, https://doi.org/10.1016/S1474-4422(12)70191-6.
14. Ian G. Morgan, Amanda N. French, Regan S. Ashby, Xining Guo, Xiaohu Ding, Mingguang He, and Kathryn A. Rose, "The Epidemic of Myopia: Aetiology and Prevention," *Progress in Retinal and Eye Research* 62 (January 2018): 134–149. https://doi.org/10.1016/j.preteyeres.2017.09.004.
15. Gloria Mark, *Attention Span: A Groundbreaking Way to Restore Balance, Happiness and Productivity* (Hanover Square Press, 2023), 174.
16. Adrian F. Ward, Kristen Duke, Ayelet Gneezy, and Maarten W. Bos, "Brain Drain: The Mere Presence of One's Own Smartphone Reduces Available Cognitive Capacity," *Journal of the Association for Consumer Research* 2, no. 2 (2017): 140–54, https://doi.org/10.1086/691462.
17. Irving John Good, "Speculations Concerning the First Ultraintelligent Machine," *Advances in Computers* 6 (1966): 31–88, https://doi.org/10.1016/S0065-2458(08)60418-0.
18. Eric Topol, *Deep Medicine: How Artificial Intelligence Can Make Healthcare Human Again* (Basic Books, 2019), 15–20, 102–105, 130–132.

19. Sigal Samuel, "Shannon Vallor Says AI Does Present an Existential Risk—but Not the One You Think," *Vox*, November 21, 2024, https://www.vox.com/future-perfect/384517/shannon-vallor-data-ai-philosophy-ethics-technology-edinburgh-future-perfect-50.
20. Sean Illing, "Is ChatGPT Killing Higher Education?," *Vox*, July 5, 2025, https://www.vox.com/the-gray-area/418793/chatgpt-claude-ai-higher-education-cheating.
21. Rolling Stone Culture Council, "AI-Generated Music: A Creative Revolution or a Cultural Crisis?" *Rolling Stone* (blog), October 15, 2024, https://council.rollingstone.com/blog/the-impact-of-ai-generated-music.
22. Ella Creamer, "Amazon Restricts Authors from Self-publishing More Than Three Books a Day After AI Concerns," *The Guardian*, September 20, 2023, https://www.theguardian.com/books/2023/sep/20/amazon-restricts-authors-from-self-publishing-more-than-three-books-a-day-after-ai-concerns.
23. Ella Creamer, "Writers Condemn Startup's Plans to Publish 8,000 Books Next Year Using AI," *The Guardian*, November 26, 2024, https://www.theguardian.com/books/2024/nov/26/writers-condemn-startups-plans-to-publish-8000-books-next-year-using-ai-spines-artificial-intelligence.
24. Lucy Knight, "US Authors Guild to Certify Books from 'Human Intellect' Rather than AI," *The Guardian*, January 30, 2023, https://www.theguardian.com/books/2025/jan/30/us-authors-guild-to-certify-books-from-human-intellect-rather-than-ai-human-authored.
25. Emad Mostaque, "The Future of AI-Generated TV Shows, Movies, and Entertainment," Reddit, May 19, 2023, www.reddit.com/r/ArtificialInteligence/comments/13lttey/the_future_of_aigenerated_tv_showsmovies_and/.

26. S. J. Velasquez, "How AI Is Bringing Film Stars Back from the Dead," *BBC*, July 18, 2023, https://www.bbc.com/future/article/20230718-how-ai-is-bringing-film-stars-back-from-the-dead.
27. Ellen Glover, "AI Influencers, Explained: Are Computer-Generated Personas Really Taking Over Social Media?," *Built In*, September 24, 2024, https://builtin.com/articles/ai-influencer.
28. Lauren Goode, "I Stared into the AI Void with the SocialAI App," *Wired*, September 18, 2024, https://www.wired.com/story/socialai-app-ai-chatbots-chatgpt.
29. Neil Sahota, "How AI Companions Are Redefining Human Relationships in the Digital Age," *Forbes*, July 18, 2024, https://www.forbes.com/sites/neilsahota/2024/07/18/how-ai-companions-are-redefining-human-relationships-in-the-digital-age.
30. "7 Key AI Investment Statistics Every Investor Should Know," *Edge Delta* (blog), May 24, 2024, https://edgedelta.com/company/blog/ai-investment-statistics.
31. Michael Chui, Eric Hazan, Roger Roberts, Nancy L. Fleischer, Alison M. Mondul, Karen McLean, Bhramar Mukherjee, and Celeste Leigh Pearce, "The Economic Potential of Generative AI: The Next Productivity Frontier," *McKinsey & Company*, June 14, 2023, https://www.mckinsey.com/capabilities/mckinsey-digital/our-insights/the-economic-potential-of-generative-ai-the-next-productivity-frontier.
32. Ailya Alimujiang, Ashley Wiensch, Johnathan Boss, Alex Singla, Kate Smaje, Alex Sukharevsky, Larina Yee, and Rodney Zemmel, "Association Between Life Purpose and Mortality Among US Adults Older Than 50 Years," *JAMA Network Open* 2, no. 5 (2019): e194270, https://doi.org/10.1001/jamanetworkopen.2019.4270.
33. Edward Gibbon, *The History of the Decline and Fall of the Roman Empire*, ed. David Womersley (Penguin Classics, 1994), 111.

34. Benjamin Franklin, *The Works of Benjamin Franklin*, Vol. 7, *Letters and Misc. Writings 1775–1779*, ed. John Bigelow (G. P. Putnam's Sons, 1904), 44, https://oll.libertyfund.org/titles/franklin-the-works-of-benjamin-franklin-vol-vii-letters-and-misc-writings-1775-1779.
35. Kaṇāda, *The Vaiśeṣika Sūtras of Kaṇāda*, trans. N. Sinha (The Indian Press, 1911), 3.
36. Horace Hayman Wilson, trans., *The Vishnu Purana: A System of Hindu Mythology and Tradition: Complete with VI Volumes* (Heritage Publishers, 2024), 7–10.
37. Zuisei Goddard, "Interdependence, Entanglement and Possibility," Ocean Mind Sangha, March 15, 2022, https://oceanmindsangha.org/articles/entanglement-possibility-zuisei-goddard.
38. F. Sherwood Taylor, *A Short History of Science and Scientific Thought: With Readings from the Great Scientists from the Babylonians to Einstein* (W. W. Norton & Company, 1949), 34–36.
39. Devrishi, "The Sound Cosmos Inquiry—Part 1: Philosophical Foundations," SSNR (May 22, 2025), https://doi.org/10.2139/ssrn.5264495.
40. Yibing Shen, Lu Wang, Enwei Zhang, and Xinyi Zhang, "The Relationship Between Nervous System and Meridians," *Highlights in Science, Engineering and Technology* 36 (March 2023): 509–516, http://dx.doi.org/10.54097/hset.v36i.5723.
41. Mahatma Gandhi, *The Wit and Wisdom of Gandhi*, ed. Homer A. Jack (Dover Publications, 2005), 59.

Chapter 1
Human 2.0: How the AI Revolution Can Create a Leap Forward in Human Evolution

1. G. Michael Hopf, *Those Who Remain: A Postapocalyptic Novel* (CreateSpace Independent Publishing, 2016), Author's Note.

2. Malala Yousafzai and Christina Lamb, *I Am Malala: The Girl Who Stood Up for Education and Was Shot by the Taliban* (Little, Brown and Company, 2013), 117–56.
3. Helen Keller, *The Story of My Life* (General Press, 2025).
4. Malidoma Patrice Somé, *Of Water and the Spirit: Ritual, Magic, and Initiation in the Life of an African Shaman* (Putnam Books, 1994), 223–225.
5. Teresa Keast, "The Spiritual Awakening of the Third Eye," *Quest* 111:1 (Winter 2023): 31–35, https://www.theosophical.org/publications/quest-magazine/the-spiritual -awakening-of-the-third-eye.
6. Nassim Nicholas Taleb, *Antifragile: Things That Gain from Disorder* (Random House, 2012), 3.
7. Kelly McGonigal, *The Upside of Stress: Why Stress Is Good for You, and How to Get Good at It* (Avery 2015), 50–51.
8. Mark P. Mattson, "Hormesis Defined," *Ageing Research Reviews* 7, no. 1 (2008): 1–7, http://dx.doi.org/10.1016/j.arr.2007.08.007.
9. Richard G. Tedeschi and Lawrence G. Calhoun, "Posttraumatic Growth: Conceptual Foundations and Empirical Evidence," *Psychological Inquiry* 15, no. 1 (2009): 1–18, https://doi.org/10.1207/s15327965pli1501_01.
10. Matt Puderbaugh and Prabhu D. Emmady, "Neuroplasticity," *StatPearls*, (May 1, 2023), https://www.ncbi.nlm.nih.gov/books/NBK557811/.
11. Swami Prabhavananda and Frederick Manchester, trans., *The Upanishads: Breath of the Eternal* (Vedanta Press, 1947), 91.
12. Swami Sivananda, trans. *The Bhagavad Gita* (The Divine Life Trust Society, 1984), chapter 6, verse 5.
13. Lao Tzu, *Tao Te Ching*, trans. Stephen Mitchell (Harper & Row, 1988), 34.
14. Bruce S. McEwen and Peter J. Gianaros, "Stress- and Allostasis-Induced Brain Plasticity," *Annual Review of Medicine* 62 (February 2011): 431–45, https://doi.org/10.1146/annurev-med-052209-100430.

15. Christopher G. Davey and Ben J. Harrison, "The Brain's Center of Gravity: How the Default Mode Network Helps Us to Understand the Self," *World Psychiatry* 17, no. 2 (2018): 278–79, https://doi.org/10.1002/wps.20553.
16. Randy L. Buckner and Lauren M. DiNicola, "The Brain's Default Network: Updated Anatomy, Physiology and Evolving Insights," *Nature Reviews Neuroscience* 20, no. 10 (2019): 593–608, https://www.nature.com/articles/s41583-019-0212-7.
17. Lao Tzu, *Tao Te Ching*.
18. Luke 17:33 (New Living Translation).

Chapter 2
AI Will Think for You: Think for Yourself

1. Tali Sharot, *The Optimism Bias: A Tour of the Irrationally Positive Brain* (Pantheon, 2011), 4.
2. Steven Pinker, *Enlightenment Now: The Case for Reason, Science, Humanism, and Progress* (Viking, 2018).
3. Anne Case and Angus Deaton, *Deaths of Despair and the Future of Capitalism* (Princeton University Press, 2020), 3.
4. Wendy Wood and Dennis Rünger, "Psychology of Habit," *Annual Review of Psychology* 67 (September 10, 2015): 289–314, https://doi.org/10.1146/annurev-psych-122414-033417.
5. Anne Craig, "Discovery of 'Thought Worms' Opens Window to the Mind," *Queen's Gazette*, July 13, 2020, https://www.queensu.ca/gazette/stories/discovery-thought-worms-opens-window-mind.
6. Joseph O'Connor and John Seymour, *Introducing NLP: Psychological Skills for Understanding and Influencing People* (Thorsons, 1990), 22.
7. Joe Dispenza, *Breaking the Habit of Being Yourself: How to Lose Your Mind and Create a New One* (Hay House, 2012).

8. DeepMind, "AlphaGo: Mastering the Ancient Game of Go with Machine Learning," Google, accessed March 20, 2025, https://deepmind.com/research/highlighted-research/alphago.
9. John Jumper, Richard Evans, Alexander Pritzel, Tim Green, Michael Figurnov, Olaf Romeberger, Kathryn Tunyasuvunakool, et al., "Highly Accurate Protein Structure Prediction with AlphaFold." *Nature* 596 (August 26, 2021): 583–89, https://doi.org/10.1038/s41586-021-03819-2.
10. Yuval Noah Harari, *Nexus: A Brief History of Information Networks from the Stone Age to AI* (Harper, 2024).
11. Walter Isaacson, *Einstein: His Life and Universe* (Simon & Schuster, 2007), 6.
12. Blaise Pascal, *Pensées*, trans. W. F. Trotter (E.P. Dutton, 1958), 113.
13. Nick Bostrom, "Ethical Issues in Advanced Artificial Intelligence," *Cognitive, Emotive and Ethical Aspects of Decision Making in Humans and in Artificial Intelligence*, Vol. 2, ed. I. Smit et al. (Institute of Advanced Studies in Systems Research and Cybernetics, 2003), 12–17, https://nickbostrom.com/ethics/ai.
14. Benjamin Libet, Curtis A. Gleason, Elwood W. Wright, and Dennis K. Pearl, "Time of Conscious Intention to Act in Relation to Onset of Cerebral Activity (Readiness-Potential): The Unconscious Initiation of a Freely Voluntary Act," *Brain: Oxford Academic* 106, no. 3 (1983): 623–42, https://doi.org/10.1093/brain/106.3.623.
15. Bernardo Kastrup, *The Idea of the World: A Multi-Disciplinary Argument for the Mental Nature of Reality* (Iff Books, 2019), 107–8.
16. Stephen M. Fleming and Christopher D. Frith, eds., *The Cognitive Neuroscience of Metacognition* (Springer, 2014), 1.
17. René Descartes, *Discourse on Method and Meditations on First Philosophy*, trans. Donald A. Cress (Hackett Publishing Company, 1999), 18.

Chapter 3
Robots Will Replace You: Become Irreplaceable

1. Research and Markets, "The Worldwide Industrial Robotics Industry is Expected to Reach $43.9 Billion in 2027," *GlobalNewsWire*, December 19, 2022, https://www.globenewswire.com/news-release/2022/12/19/2576051/28124/en/The-Worldwide-Industrial-Robotics-Industry-is-Expected-to-Reach-43-9-Billion-in-2027.html.
2. Madeline Stone, "Amazon Has More Than 750,000 Robots Working in Its Fulfillment Centers. Here Are Some of the Things They Can Do," *Business Insider*, February 11, 2025, https://www.businessinsider.com/how-amazon-uses-robots-sort-transport-packages-warehouses-2025-2.
3. "Restaurant Robotics: How Robots Are Changing Foodservice," Aaron Allen & Associates: Global Restaurant Consultants, accessed July 29, 2025, https://aaronallen.com/blog/restaurant-robotics.
4. Zak Ali, "Valued to Be $20.7 Billion by 2026, Medical Robots Slated for Robust Growth Worldwide," *PR Newswire*, September 2, 2021, https://www.prnewswire.com/news-releases/valued-to-be-20-7-billion-by-2026--medical-robots-slated-for-robust-growth-worldwide-301367300.html.
5. Shubhangi Goel, "Robotics Will Have a ChatGPT Moment in the Next 2 or 3 Years, Says Vinod Khosla," *Business Insider*, July 2, 2025. https://www.businessinsider.com/robotics-chatgpt-moment-in-the-next-few-years-vinod-khosla-2025-7.
6. James Lambert and Edward Cone, "How Robots Change the World: What Automation Really Means for Jobs and Productivity," *Oxford Economics*, June 2019, https://www.oxfordeconomics.com/resource/how-robots-change-the-world/.
7. Amanda Russo, "Recession and Automation Changes Our Future of Work, but There Are Jobs Coming, Report Says," *World Economic*

Forum Press Release, October 20, 2020, https://www.weforum.org/press/2020/10/recession-and-automation-changes-our-future-of-work-but-there-are-jobs-coming-report-says-52c5162fce/.

8. Richard Mudge, David Montgomery, Erica Groshen, John Paul Macduffie, Susan Helper, and Charles Carson, "America's Workforce and the Self-Driving Future: Realizing Productivity Gains and Spurring Economic Growth," *Securing America's Future Energy*, June 2018, https://avworkforce.secureenergy.org/wp-content/uploads/2018/06/Americas-Workforce-and-the-Self-Driving-Future_Realizing-Productivity-Gains-and-Spurring-Economic-Growth.pdf.
9. Malcolm Foster, "Aging Japan: Robots May Have Role in Future of Elder Care," *Reuters*, March 27, 2018, https://www.reuters.com/article/us-japan-ageing-robots-idUSKBN1H33AB.
10. Eliza Gregory Wilkins, *The Delphic Maxims in Literature* (Hassell Street Press, 2021), 2.
11. Plato, "Apology of Socrates," in *Plato: Five Dialogues*, trans. G. M. A. Grube and John M. Cooper (Hackett Publishing Company, 2002), 41.
12. Randall V. Bass and J. W. Good, "Educare and Educere: Is a Balance Possible in the Educational System?" *The Educational Forum* 68, no. 2 (2004): 161–68. https://doi.org/10.1080/00131720408984623.
13. Walter Isaacson, *Steve Jobs* (Simon & Schuster, 2011), 49.
14. Howard Thurman, *The Living Wisdom of Howard Thurman: A Visionary for Our Time* (Monk Publishing, 1995), 48–49.

Chapter 4

AI Progress Will Outpace You: Become a Visionary

1. Tees Valley Museums Group, "John Walker and the Friction Match," *Tees Valley Museums* (blog), accessed May 19, 2025, https://teesvalleymuseums.org/blog/post/john-walker-and-the-friction-match/.

2. Stephen R. Covey, *The 8th Habit: From Effectiveness to Greatness* (Free Press, 2004), 85.
3. Thomas Carlyle, *On Heroes, Hero-Worship, and the Heroic in History: Rethinking the Western Tradition*, ed. David R. Sorensen and Brent E. Kiser (Yale University Press, 2013).
4. Martin Luther King Jr., *A Knock at Midnight: Inspiration from the Great Sermons of Reverend Martin Luther King*, Jr., ed. Clayborne Carson and Peter Holloran (Grand Central Publishing, 1998), 170–71.
5. John F. Kennedy, "Address at Rice University on the Nation's Space Effort," September 12, 1962, Houston, Texas, John F. Kennedy Presidential Library and Museum, https://www.jfklibrary.org/archives/other-resources/john-f-kennedy-speeches/rice-university-19620912.
6. Nelson Mandela, *Long Walk to Freedom: The Autobiography of Nelson Mandela* (Back Bay Books, 1995).
7. Matthew Restall, *Seven Myths of the Spanish Conquest* (Oxford University Press, 2021).
8. Roger E. Beaty, Mathias Benedek, Paul J. Silvia, and Daniel L. Schacter, "Creative Cognition and Brain Network Dynamics," *Trends in Cognitive Sciences* 20, no. 2 (2016): 87–95, https://doi.org/10.1016/j.tics.2015.10.004.
9. Jim Collins and Jerry I. Porras, *Built to Last: Successful Habits of Visionary Companies* (Harper Business, 1994), 204–8.
10. Archimedes, "On the Equilibrium of Planes," T*he Works of Archimedes*, trans. and ed. T. L. Heath (Cambridge University Press, 1897), 189–220, https://www.aproged.pt/biblioteca/worksofarchimede.pdf.
11. Vilfredo Pareto, *Cours d'économie Politique* (F. Rouge, 1896), 371–86.
12. Frances Maidment, ed., *Pablo Picasso: A Retrospective* (Thames & Hudson, 2019), 34–35.
13. Barbara Goldsmith, *Obsessive Genius: The Inner World of Marie Curie* (W. W. Norton, 2005).

14. James Clear, *Atomic Habits: An Easy & Proven Way to Build Good Habits & Break Bad Ones* (Avery, 2018).
15. Walter Isaacson, *Steve Jobs* (Simon & Schuster, 2011), 328–331.
16. Kitty Kelley, *Oprah: A Biography* (Crown Archetype, 2010), 471.
17. Michelangelo Buonarroti, *Complete Poems and Selected Letters of Michelangelo*, ed. Robert N. Liscott, trans. Creighton Gilbert (Princeton University Press, 1980), 456–57.
18. David Epstein, *Range: Why Generalists Triumph in a Specialized World* (Riverhead Books, 2019).
19. Louise Axon, Elisa Friedman, and Janice Molloy, "Leading for Today and Tomorrow: Capabilities for a Changing World," Harvard Business Publishing, 2019, https://www.harvardbusiness.org/wp-content/uploads/2019/09/21325_CL_LeadershipCapabilities_White_Paper_Digital_Sept2019.pdf.
20. Walter Isaacson, *Leonardo da Vinci* (Simon & Schuster, 2017).
21. Michael Peña, "Steve Jobs to 2005 Graduates: 'Stay Hungry, Stay Foolish,'" *Stanford Report*, June 12, 2005, news.stanford.edu/2005/06/14/jobs-061505/.
22. Walter Isaacson, *Benjamin Franklin: An American Life* (Simon & Schuster, 2004).
23. Marie Curie, *Radioactive Substances* (Dover Publications, 2002).
24. Jonathon Keats, *You Belong to the Universe: Buckminster Fuller and the Future* (Oxford University Press, 2016).
25. Neal Gabler, *Walt Disney: The Triumph of the American Imagination* (Knopf, 2006).
26. Clear, *Atomic Habits*, 207.
27. "Quotes Falsely Attributed to Winston Churchill," The International Churchill Society, January 17, 2023, winstonchurchill.org/resources/quotes/quotes-falsely-attributed/.
28. Angela L. Duckworth, Christopher Peterson, Michael D. Matthews, and Dennis R. Kelly, "Grit: Perseverance and Passion for Long-Term

Goals," *Journal of Personality and Social Psychology* 92, no. 6 (2007): 1087–1101, https://pubmed.ncbi.nlm.nih.gov/17547490/.

29. Kennedy, "Address at Rice University."
30. Malala Yousafzai and Christina Lamb, *I Am Malala: The Girl Who Stood Up for Education and Was Shot by the Taliban* (Little, Brown and Company, 2013), 230–250.
31. J. K. Rowling, "The Fringe Benefits of Failure, and the Importance of Imagination," June 5, 2008, Harvard University, https://news.harvard.edu/gazette/story/2008/06/text-of-j-k-rowling-speech/.
32. Frank Lewis Dyer and Thomas Commerford Martin, *Edison: His Life and Inventions* (Nova Science, 2018), 125.
33. Fred R. Shapiro, ed., *The Yale Book of Quotations* (Yale University Press, 2006), 274.
34. Joseph LeDoux, *The Emotional Brain: The Mysterious Underpinnings of Emotional Life* (Simon & Schuster, 1996).
35. Romans 12:2 (New Revised Standard Version).

Chapter 5
Deepfakes Will Deceive You: Live by Insight Not Eyesight

1. Prarthana Prakash, "A Deepfake 'CFO' Tricked the British Design Firm behind the Sydney Opera House in $25 Million Scam," *Fortune*, May 17, 2024, https://fortune.com/europe/2024/05/17/arup-deepfake-fraud-scam-victim-hong-kong-25-million-cfo/.
2. Jesse Damiani, "A Voice Deepfake Was Used to Scam a CEO out of $243,000," *Forbes*, September 3, 2019, https://www.forbes.com/sites/jessedamiani/2019/09/03/a-voice-deepfake-was-used-to-scam-a-ceo-out-of-243000/.
3. Geri Weis-Corbley, "Attorney Warns His Voice was Cloned by AI in Phone Scam That Nearly Tricked His Dad Out of $35k," *Good News Network*, October 13, 2024, https://www.goodnewsnetwork.org/

attorney-warns-his-voice-was-cloned-by-ai-in-phone-scam-that-nearly-tricked-his-dad-out-of-35k.

4. Tali Sharot, *The Optimism Bias: A Tour of the Irrationally Positive Brain* (Pantheon, 2011), 163–66.
5. Aristotle, *Metaphysics*, trans. W. D. Ross, The Internet Classics Archive, accessed May 20, 2025, https://classics.mit.edu/Aristotle/meta physics .4.iv.html.
6. William Miller, "Death of a Genius: His Fourth Dimension, Time, Overtakes Einstein," *Life Magazine* 38, no. 18 (May 2, 1955): 64, https://books.google.com/books?id=dlYEAAAAMBAJ&pg=PA64.
7. Matthew 13:13 (New International Version).
8. Acharya Buddharakkhita, trans., *The Dhammapada* (Buddhist Publication Society, 2019), 3.
9. Lao Tzu, *Tao Te Ching*, trans. Stephen Mitchell (Harper & Row, 1988), 47.
10. Daniel Kahneman, *Thinking, Fast and Slow* (Farrar, Straus and Giroux, 2011).
11. Helena Petrovna Blavatsky, *The Secret Doctrine: The Synthesis of Science, Religion, and Philosophy*, Vol. 2, *Anthropogenesis* (Theosophical Publishing House, 1893), 302-20, https://www.google.com/books /edition/The_Secret_Doctrine/59s_AQAAMAAJ?hl=en&gbpv=0.
12. Matt Puderbaugh and Prabhu D. Emmady, "Neuroplasticity," National Center for Biotechnology Information: *National Library of Medicine*, updated May 1, 2023, https://www.ncbi.nlm.nih.gov/books /NBK557811/.
13. Nicholas Carr, *The Shallows: What the Internet Is Doing to Our Brains* (W. W. Norton & Company, 2010), 114–22.
14. Idries Shah, *The Exploits of the Incomparable Mulla Nasrudin* (Octagon Press, 1983), 9.
15. Carl Gustav Jung, *Two Essays on Analytical Psychology*, trans. R. F. C. Hull (Routledge, 1999).

16. Iamblichus, *The Life of Pythagoras*, trans. Thomas Taylor (Inner Traditions, 1986).
17. Thomas Heath, *A History of Greek Mathematics*, Vol. 1, *From Thales to Euclid* (Dover Publications, 1981).
18. Britta K. Hölzel, James Carmody, Mark Vangel, Christina Congleton, Sita M. Yerramsetti, Tim Gard, and Sara W. Lazar, "Mindfulness Practice Leads to Increases in Regional Brain Gray Matter Density," *Psychiatry Research: Neuroimaging* 191, no. 1 (2011): 36–43, https://doi.org/10.1016/j.pscychresns.2010.08.006.
19. Norman Doidge, *The Brain That Changes Itself: Stories of Personal Triumph from the Frontiers of Brain Science* (Viking Press, 2007), 20–21.

Chapter 6
AI Will Expose You: Become Transparent

1. Olivia-Anne Cleary, "Robbie Williams Confronts His Darkest Moments in New Netflix Documentary," *Time*, November 8, 2023, https://time.com/6332204/robbie-williams-netflix-documentary-revelations/.
2. Maria Mercedes Lara and Melody Chiu, "Kevin Hart Apologizes to His Wife and Kids in Emotional Video After Alleged Extortion: 'I'm Not Perfect,'" *People*, September 16, 2017, https://people.com/celebrity/kevin-hart-apologizes-eniko-parrish-extortion-video/.
3. Michal Kosinski, David Stillwell, and Thore Graepel, "Private Traits and Attributes are Predictable from Digital Records of Human Behavior," *Proceedings of the National Academy of Sciences* 110, no. 15 (2013): 5802–5, https://doi.org/10.1073/pnas.1218772110.
4. Brené Brown, *Daring Greatly: How the Courage to Be Vulnerable Transforms the Way We Live, Love, Parent, and Lead* (Avery, 2012), 33.
5. Carl R. Rogers, *On Becoming a Person: A Therapist's View of Psychotherapy*, (Houghton Mifflin Harcourt, 1995), 283–84.

6. John Bowlby, *A Secure Base: Parent-Child Attachment and Healthy Human Development* (Basic Books, 1988).
7. Carl G. Jung, *The Archetypes and the Collective Unconscious*, trans. R. F. C. Hull, (Princeton University Press, 1981), 284–85.
8. Kristin Neff, *Self-Compassion: Stop Beating Yourself Up and Leave Insecurity Behind* (William Morrow, 2015).
9. Michael Slepian, *The Secret Life of Secrets: How Our Inner Worlds Shape Well-Being, Relationships, and Who We Are* (Crown, 2022), 205–41.
10. James W. Pennebaker, *Opening Up by Writing It Down: How Expressive Writing Improves Health and Eases Emotional Pain* (The Guilford Press, 2016).

Chapter 7
AI Will Widen the Wealth Gap: Build an Abundance Mindset

1. Sara Blakely, "How Spanx Got Started: Sara Blakely on How She Came Up with the Idea of Spanx Footless Pantyhose." December 1, 2011, Inc. Women's Summit, New York, NY, transcript and video, https://www.inc.com/sara-blakely/how-sara-blakley-started-spanx.html.
2. Thomas Piketty, *Capital in the Twenty-First Century*, trans. Arthur Goldhammer (Harvard University Press, 2014), 20–27.
3. Matthew 6:26–29 (King James Version).
4. Bhikkhu Bodhi, *The Noble Eightfold Path: The Way to the End of Suffering* (Buddhist Publication Society, 2020), 63–86.
5. Lao Tzu, *Tao Te Ching*, trans. Stephen Mitchell (Harper & Row, 1988), 34.
6. Robert Browning, *The Paracelsus of Robert Browning* (Baker & Taylor, 1911), 88.
7. Marvin W. Meyer, ed., *The Nag Hammadi Scriptures: The Revised and Updated Translation of Sacred Gnostic Text* (HarperOne, 2009), 148.

8. Derek Rydall, *Emergence: Seven Steps for Radical Life Change* (Beyond Words/Atria Books, 2015), 6.
9. Derek Rydall, *The Abundance Project: 40 Days to More Wealth, Health, Love, and Happiness* (Beyond Words/Atria Books, 2018), 13.
10. Y. Alegria Robelly Espinoza, "Barter, Old Fashioned or a Modern Alternative?" (master's thesis, Wageningen University, 2019), https://edepot.wur.nl/509772.
11. David Harvey, *The New Imperialism* (Oxford University Press, 2003), 26–32.
12. "Origin and History of *Currency*," etymonline, www.etymonline.com/word/currency.
13. N. Gregory Mankiw, *Principles of Economics*, 9th ed. (Cengage Learning, 2020), 251.
14. N. Gregory Mankiw, *Macroeconomics*, 10th ed. (Worth Publishers, 2018), 136.
15. Eric Rauchway, *The Great Depression and the New Deal: A Very Short Introduction* (Oxford University Press, 2008), 16–17.
16. Jack Canfield and Janet Switzer, *The Success Principles* (William Morrow, 2005), 189.
17. Robert Browning, *The Paracelsus*, 88.
18. Bruce H. Lipton, *The Biology of Belief: Unleashing the Power of Consciousness, Matter & Miracles* (Hay House, 2005), 72.

Chapter 8
AI Will Commoditize You: Become the Artist of Your Life

1. Walter Isaacson, *Leonardo da Vinci* (Simon & Schuster, 2017).
2. Fyodor Dostoevsky, *The Idiot*, trans. Henry and Olga Carlisle (Signet Classics, 2003), 313.
3. Rumi, *The Essential Rumi*, trans. Coleman Barks and John Moyne (HarperOne, 2004), 36.

4. Peter Burke, *The Italian Renaissance: Culture and Society in Italy* (Princeton University Press, 2014).
5. William Blake, "Auguries of Innocence," in *The Complete Poetry and Prose of William Blake*, rev. ed., ed. David V. Erdman, (University of California Press, 1982), 493.
6. Burke, *The Italian Renaissance.*
7. Genesis 1:26–27 (New Revised Standard Version).
8. "National Beer Sales & Production Data," Brewers Association, accessed May 20, 2024, www.brewersassociation.org/statistics-and-data/national-beer-stats/.
9. "Number of Active Etsy Inc. Sellers from 2012 to 2024" Statista, March 26, 2025, https://www.statista.com/statistics/409374/etsy-annual-revenue/.
10. Ray Oldenburg, *The Great Good Place: Cafes, Coffee Shops, Bookstores, Bars, Hair Salons, and Other Hangouts at the Heart of a Community* (Da Capo Press, 1999), 16.
11. B. Joseph Pine and James H. Gilmore, *The Experience Economy: Competing for Customer Time, Attention, and Money* (Harvard Business Review Press, 2019), 2–3.
12. Cody Skonord, "Post-it Notes: An Employee Idea That Was Originally a Mistake," Ideawake, February 19, 2021, https://ideawake.com/post-it-notes-employee-idea-that-was-originally-mistake/.
13. Marie Kondo, *The Life-Changing Magic of Tidying Up: The Japanese Art of Decluttering and Organizing* (Ten Speed Press, 2014).
14. Shoshana Zuboff. *The Age of Surveillance Capitalism: The Fight for a Human Future at the New Frontier of Power* (PublicAffairs, 2019).
15. Robert B. Cialdini, *Influence: The Psychology of Persuasion*, rev. ed., (Harper Business, 2021), 17.

Chapter 9
AI Will Weaponize Intimacy: Upgrade Your Heartware

1. René A. Spitz, "Hospitalism: An Inquiry into the Genesis of Psychiatric Conditions in Early Childhood," *The Psychoanalytic Study of the Child* 1, no. 1 (2017): 53–74, https://doi.org/10.1080/00797308.1945.11823126.
2. Robert M. Nerem, Murina J. Levesque, and J. Frederick Cornhill, "Social Environment as a Factor in Diet-Induced Atherosclerosis," *Science* 208, no. 4451 (1980): 1475–76, https://doi.org/10.1126/science.7384790.
3. Tiffany Field, *Touch* (MIT Press, 2001), 37.
4. Julianne Holt-Lunstad, Timothy B. Smith, and J. Bradley Layton, "Social Relationships and Mortality Risk: A Meta-analytic Review," *PLoS Medicine* 7, no. 7 (2010), https://doi.org/10.1371/journal.pmed.1000316
5. Sigal Samuel, "People Are Falling in Love with—and Getting Addicted to—AI Voices," *Vox*, August 19, 2024, https://www.vox.com/future-perfect/367188/love-addicted-ai-voice-human-gpt4-emotion.
6. Philip Zimbardo and Nikita Coulombe, *Man, Interrupted: Why Young Men Are Struggling and What We Can Do About It* (Conari Press, 2016), 111.
7. World Health Organization. "Social Connection Linked to Improved Health and Reduced Risk of Early Death," *WHO*, June 30, 2025, https://www.who.int/news/item/30-06-2025-social-connection-linked-to-improved-heath-and-reduced-risk-of-early-death.
8. Jean M. Twenge, Thomas E. Joiner, Megan L. Rogers, and Gabrielle N. Martin, "Increases in Depressive Symptoms, Suicide-Related Outcomes, and Suicide Rates Among U.S. Adolescents After 2010 and Links to Increased New Media Screen Time," *Clinical Psychological Science* 6, no. 1 (2017): 3–17, https://doi.org/10.1177/2167702617723376.

9. Nazanin Andalibi and Justin Buss, "The Human in Emotion Recognition on Social Media: Attitudes, Outcomes, Risks," *CHI '20: Proceedings of the 2020 CHI Conference on Human Factors in Computing Systems* (April 23, 2020): 1-16, https://dl.acm.org/doi/10.1145/3313831.3376680.
10. Daniel Susser, Beate Roessler, and Helen Nissenbaum, "Online Manipulation: Hidden Influences in a Digital World," *Georgetown Law Technology Review* 4, no. 1 (2020): 1–45. https://doi.org/10.2139/ssrn.3306006.
11. Clare Duffy, "'There Are No Guardrails.' This Mom Believes an AI Chatbot Is Responsible for Her Son's Suicide," *CNN Business*, October 30, 2024, https://www.cnn.com/2024/10/30/tech/teen-suicide -character-ai-lawsuit.
12. Charles Dickens, *A Christmas Carol* (Chapman & Hall, 1843).
13. Dr. Seuss, *How the Grinch Stole Christmas!* (Random House, 1957).
14. *E.T. the Extra-Terrestrial*, directed by Steven Spielberg, (Universal Pictures, 1982).
15. Ovid, *Metamorphoses*, trans. David Raeburn, (Penguin Books, 2004), Book 10.
16. Richard H. Wilkinson, *The Complete Gods and Goddesses of Ancient Egypt* (Thames & Hudson, 2003), 84.
17. Georg Feuerstein, *The Yoga Tradition: Its History, Literature, Philosophy and Practice* (Hohm Press, 2001), 240-244.
18. Roger T. Ames and Henry Rosemont Jr., *The Analects of Confucius: A Philosophical Translation* (Ballantine Books, 1998), 123–126.
19. Annemarie Schimmel, *Mystical Dimensions of Islam* (University of North Carolina Press, 1975), 137.
20. Rumi, *The Essential Rumi*, trans. Coleman Barks (HarperSanFrancisco, 1995), 196.

21. J. Andrew Armour, *Neurocardiology—Anatomical and Functional Principles*, Institute of HeartMath, 2003, https://neuroimaginalinstitute.com/wp-content/uploads/2013/03/Neurocardiology.pdf.
22. Rollin McCraty and Doc Childre, "Coherence: Bridging Personal, Social, and Global Health," *Alternative Therapies* 5, no 4 (2010): 10–24, https://www.heartmath.org/assets/uploads/2015/01/coherence-bridging-personal-social-global-health.pdf.
23. Pierre Teilhard de Chardin, *The Heart of Matter*, trans. René Hague (Harcourt, 1978), 92.
24. Viktor E. Frankl, *Man's Search for Meaning* (Beacon Press, 2006), 37.
25. Nelson Mandela, *Long Walk to Freedom: The Autobiography of Nelson Mandela* (Back Bay Books, 1995).

Chapter 10
AI Will Increase Powerlessness: Reclaim Your Soul Power

1. Nelson Mandela, *Long Walk to Freedom: The Autobiography of Nelson Mandela* (Back Bay Books, 1995), 328–330.
2. William Ernest Henley, *A Book of Verses* (David Nutt, 1888), 57.
3. Mandela, *Long Walk to Freedom*, 331–363.
4. Yuval Noah Harari, *Homo Deus: A Brief History of Tomorrow* (Harper Perennial, 2017).
5. David H. Hubel, *Eye, Brain, and Vision* (W. H. Freeman & Company, 1988), 6.
6. David M. Howard and Jamie A. S. Angus, *Acoustics and Psychoacoustics*, 5th ed. (Routledge, 2017), 6.
7. "The Nobel Prize in Physics 2022," NobelPrize.org, accessed May 19, 2022, https://www.nobelprize.org/prizes/physics/2022/summary/.

8. Donald D. Hoffman, *The Case Against Reality: How Evolution Hid the Truth from Our Eyes* (Penguin, 2020), 9–10.
9. Bruce Hood, *The Self Illusion: How the Social Brain Creates Identity* (Oxford University Press, 2012), 2–3, 24–25, 44–46, 61–62.
10. John 18:36 (King James Version).
11. Thomas Byrom, trans., *The Dhammapada: The Sayings of the Buddha* (Shambhala, 1993), 3–5, 14–17, 43–45.
12. Lao Tzu, *Tao Te Ching*, trans. Stephen Mitchell (Harper & Row, 1988), 1–3, 8–9, 42–45, 106–107.
13. Plato, *The Republic*, trans. G. M. A. Grube, ed. C. D. C. Reeve (Hackett Publishing, 1992), 193–200.

Chapter 11
AI Will Divide Us: Build Community

1. Elizabeth Mehren, "And the Quartet Played On," *The Immigrant Story*, November 6, 2020, https://theimmigrantstory.org/and-the-quartet-played-on.
2. Zlata Filipović, *Zlata's Diary: A Child's Life in Sarajevo* (Viking Penguin, 1994), 33–36, 67–69, 91–93, 102–104.
3. Adrien Fillon, "'Culture Saved Us' in Besieged Sarajevo: Art as Resistance," Balkan Transitional Justice, April 4, 2025, https://balkaninsight.com/2025/04/04/culture-saved-us-in-besieged-sarajevo-art-as-resistance/.
4. Robert Waldinger and Marc Schulz, *The Good Life: Lessons from the World's Longest Scientific Study of Happiness* (Simon & Schuster, 2023), 85–89, 127–130.
5. Dan Buettner, *The Blue Zones Challenge: A 4-Week Plan for a Longer, Better Life* (National Geographic, 2021).

6. Frances Fox Piven and Richard A. Cloward, *Poor People's Movements: Why They Succeed, How They Fail* (Vintage Books, 1979), 52–58.
7. Sundar Pichai and Julie Sweet, "Passion and Partnership Are Helping Refugees in the U.S.—but We Need More," *Time*, June 20, 2023, https://time.com/6288374/helping-refugees-to-the-u-s-welcome/
8. Matthew 18:20 (New American Standard 1977 Version).
9. Martin Luther King Jr., *Where Do We Go from Here: Chaos or Community?* (Beacon Press, 2010), 16–17.
10. Peter Burke, *The Italian Renaissance: Culture and Society in Italy*, 2nd ed. (Princeton University Press, 1999), 17, 141, 271.
11. Peter Biskind, *Easy Riders, Raging Bulls: How the Sex-Drugs-and-Rock 'N Roll Generation Saved Hollywood* (Simon & Schuster, 1999), 17–19, 27–30, 49–55, 91–95.
12. Stéphane Courtois, Nicolas Werth, Jean-Louis Panné, Andrzej Paczowski, Karel Bartosek, and Jean-Louis Margolin, *The Black Book of Communism: Crimes, Terror, Repression* (Harvard University Press, 1999), 2–4, 729–730.
13. Iain McGilchrist, *The Master and His Emissary: The Divided Brain and the Making of the Western World* (Yale University Press, 2009), 6–7.
14. Philip N. Howard and Muzammil M. Hussain, *Democracy's Fourth Wave? Digital Media and the Arab Spring* (Oxford University Press, 2013), 2–3, 18–19.
15. "The Farm Today—A Model Community," The Farm Community, https://thefarmcommunity.com/the-farm-today-a-model-community/.
16. "About Us," Findhorn Foundation, https://www.findhorn.org/about-us.
17. Ben Weinberg, "The Case Against Hyper-Individualism," *Medium*, June 28, 2023, https://benjweinberg.medium.com/the-case-against-hyper-individualism-47031784ad0f.
18. "What Is the Network State?" *Hexn* (blog), June 12, 2024, https://hexn.io/blog/what-is-the-network-state-1545.

Resources

This book is just the beginning. The real transformation happens as you put these ideas into practice and join a community of people committed to becoming the kind of humans the future can't live without.

I've created spaces, tools, and trainings to help you deepen the work in this book, so you can uplevel your life, work, relationships, and so much more—no matter what changes come. These resources will keep you supported every step of the way.

The Main Hub

Your gateway to exclusive resources:

- A custom GPT guide to walk with you through the book.
- A curated library of the latest AI tools to future-proof your work and creativity.
- Ongoing practices, updates, and bonus content to help you live as a whole new human.

A Whole New Human Portal:
DerekRydall.com/WholeNewHuman

The Podcast

Tune in for inspiration, teachings, and conversations that remind you you're not alone in this journey:

Emergence: A Revolutionary Path for Radical Life Change:
podcasts.apple.com/us/podcast/emergence
-a-revolutionary-path-for-radical-life/id878870353

Podcast Portal:
DerekRydall.com/podcasts

Special Gift

Decode your deepest purpose to heal your life and fulfill your dreams:

Life Work Breakthrough:
Members.DerekRydall.com/the-life-code-discover-life-story

Trainings, Videos, and Workshops

Practical, transformational sessions on abundance, purpose, and building the future you want—starting now:

Free Trainings & Workshops:
DerekRydall.com/free-trainings

Dozens of trainings to help you navigate the AI era, embody your purpose, and step boldly into the life you were born to live:

Legendary Life YouTube Channel:
youtube.com/@DerekRydall-YourLegendaryLife

Stay Connected

Find events, workshops, and online gatherings where we rise together:

- Website: DerekRydall.com
- Community: DerekRydall.com/events
- @DerekRydall
- @drydall
- @derekrydall

My Other Books

Learn more about my previous books and find additional bonus material:

Emergence: Seven Steps For Radical Life Change:
www.GetEmergenceBook.com

The Abundance Project: 40 Days to More Wealth, Health, Love, and Happiness:
TheAbundanceProjectBook.com

This is more than a book, it's a movement. Every time you reclaim your true identity, every time you choose purpose over programming, every time you let yourself become more fully alive—you're not just changing yourself, you're helping to reshape the future of humanity.

Welcome to the path of becoming a whole new human.